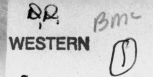

OTHER BOOKS BY AL LACY

Angel of Mercy series:
  A Promise for Breanna (Book One)
  Faithful Heart (Book Two)
  Captive Set Free (Book Three)
  A Dream Fulfilled (Book Four)

Journeys of the Stranger series:
  Legacy (Book One)
  Silent Abduction (Book Two)
  Blizzard (Book Three)
  Tears of the Sun (Book Four)
  Circle of Fire (Book Five)

Battles of Destiny (Civil War series):
  Beloved Enemy (Battle of First Bull Run)
  A Heart Divided (Battle of Mobile Bay)
  A Promise Unbroken (Battle of Rich Mountain)
  Shadowed Memories (Battle of Shiloh)
  Joy from Ashes (Battle of Fredericksburg)
  Season of Valor (Battle of Gettysburg)

QUIET THUNDER

AL LACY

MULTNOMAH BOOKS

QUIET THUNDER
© 1996 by Lew A. Lacy

published by Multnomah Books
a part of the Questar publishing family

Edited by Rodney L. Morris and
Deena Davis
Cover design by David Uttley
Cover illustration by Sergio Martínez

International Standard Book Number: 0-88070-975-8

Printed in the United States of America.

For information:
Questar Publishers, Inc.
Post Office Box 1720
Sisters, Oregon 97759

96 97 98 99 00 01 02 03 04 05 — 10 9 8 7 6 5 4 3 2 1

In loving memory of my father-in-law,
Sam Claiborne,
who was ushered into the arms of Jesus in 1982.

As a Cherokee Indian, he epitomized the
American Indians in this story...
quiet, deep-thinking, and a man of his word.

PROLOGUE

———◆———

American history has recorded no more fierce and dramatic conflict than the battles between red man and white on the plains, in the deserts, and in the mountains and forests of the American West during the nineteenth century.

Buffalo hunters, trappers, emigrants, soldiers, and all the other white men who came west, killing the game, cutting down the trees, and claiming land for themselves—with no regard for the Indians who had lived there from time immemorial—became reason for all-out war in the minds of the red men.

The Indian warrior, fighting for his land, hunted white men much as he hunted big game. He was expert at luring unsuspecting animals or "white-eyes" enemies into an ambush. He was especially skilled in concealing his own presence. As the tough old frontiersman Jim Bridger once said, "Where there ain't no Injuns, you'll find 'em the thickest."

Certainly no opposing forces ever differed more radically than the United States Army and the hostile Indians of the West in the years 1850-1890. The military leaders were professional soldiers who had studied the monumental battles of world history at West Point. A great number of them had gained invaluable experience on the battlefields of the Mexican War in midcentury, and an even greater number had learned clever military tactics during the Civil War.

Yet the rough and rugged leaders of the hostile Indian tribes they encountered were hard-nosed, stubborn, intelligent warriors who paid no mind to the white officers' military reputations. They would not be pressured into fighting according to white man's rules, and they repeatedly embarrassed their educated opponents by defeating the soldiers sent against them.

When glory-seeking, cocky young officers, eager to earn fame on the frontier, underestimated the leadership and fighting qualities of the illiterate "savages," they invited disaster, and paid for it with their lives and the lives of the men they commanded.

Much has been written about the horrors of Indian warfare—the Indians' "heathen inclination" for torturing prisoners and mutilating the bodies of dead enemies. But these atrocities did not originate during their wars with the white invaders. Long before white settlers and soldiers overran the West, red-skinned warriors did the same thing with their inter-tribal foes. Usually these heinous actions followed a revenge raid against enemies of other tribes who had purposely killed or wounded a prominent chief.

The savagery was not limited to the practices of the red man. Uniformed soldiers were often guilty of attacking Indian villages and camps when the warriors were away. Defenseless Indian women, children, and aged men were slaughtered indiscriminately. This was not condoned by the big brass in Washington, nor even by most fort commandants, but it happened frequently without the military leaders' knowledge.

Such brutality only served to enrage the Indians, especially Red Cloud, a young Oglala Sioux sub-chief. Early in 1866, the U.S. government commissioners at Fort Laramie, Wyoming, tried to negotiate a treaty with the Sioux and Northern Cheyenne to secure right-of-way for emigrants through Indian territory. Red Cloud attended the meeting and, unknown to the white men, overheard a discussion of plans to eventually overpower the Indians and force them to live restrictive lives on reservations.

Red Cloud left the treaty meeting, declaring the whites to be exactly the fork-tongued enemies he had previously asserted them to be. He took his warriors with him and declared war.

Later in that same year, Red Cloud led a vicious attack on an army unit of eighty-one men out of Fort Laramie under the leadership of Captain William J. Fetterman. The incident became known as the "Fetterman Massacre."

Red Cloud's force was much smaller than Fetterman's, but the young warrior sub-chief had cleverly lured Fetterman and his men into an ambush. Red Cloud gained so much prestige by the defeat of the Fetterman unit that he became one of the leading war chiefs of the Sioux nation.

The pages of American history record that Red Cloud was a fierce and ruthless warrior against the white invaders of his land, but that he was a man of his word. He utterly despised a man who would not keep his word. His hatred for the white man continually festered because they were ever making promises to the Indians but never keeping them.

The Indians' hatred toward the whites grew even deeper when the U.S. government began sending more troops to the West and building more forts. By early 1876, the planned operation to place the Indians on reservations was in full force. The Sioux, Arapaho, and Cheyenne tribes rebelled fiercely.

Hunkpapa Sioux battle strategist, Chief Sitting Bull, and Oglala Sioux warrior Chief Crazy Horse united forces to fight the hated whites.

The top brass in Washington, D.C. made plans to tame the recalcitrant Indians by sending the famed Seventh Cavalry from Fort Abraham Lincoln in Dakota Territory, under the command of Brigadier General Alfred Terry.

The Seventh would rendezvous with two columns in southern Montana Territory where the Big Horn River flows out of the

Yellowstone. The columns were under the command of General George Crook and General John Gibbon.

On May 17, 1876, the expedition left Fort Abraham Lincoln. Among General Terry's officers were Captain Frederick Benteen, Major Marcus A. Reno, and Lieutenant Colonel George Armstrong Custer.

The Seventh Cavalry arrived at the rendezvous spot on June 23 and met General Gibbon's column, but General Crook had not yet shown up. Terry was unaware that Crook and his men had met up with hostile Indians at the Rosebud River on June 17, and had suffered many losses.

Terry's scouts had reported a Sioux camp in the Little Big Horn Valley, next to the Little Big Horn River. In spite of General Crook's tardiness, Terry decided to launch an attack. He divided the Seventh Cavalry, giving Custer two hundred and thirty-one men and Reno one hundred and twelve.

The plan was for the divided Seventh to converge on the Sioux camp at two angles from the south. General Terry would go with General Gibbon and his men, and come at the camp from the north. The attack was set for June 26. Terry hoped General Crook would show up by then.

When Custer's column arrived near the Sioux camp, it appeared that the Indians were few in number. Custer went against General Terry's orders and led his men in an attack on June 25. Instead of a few warriors, as Custer had guessed, there were four thousand warriors. On the grassy, wind-swept hills just east of the Little Big Horn River, Custer's division of the Seventh Cavalry was annihilated.

Out of the dust and smoke of the famous Little Big Horn battle comes the legend of Quiet Thunder, a brave and skillful warrior of the Oglala Sioux, and the man who influenced his life more than any other—John Stranger.

This is Quiet Thunder's story.

❖

ONE

The rolling hills of western Nebraska Territory in late May shimmered beneath the sun's burning gaze.

Fire Eagle stood at the edge of the village and watched a band of fellow warriors, led by his father, Gray Shadow, ride north to hunt buffalo. He could see veteran sub-chiefs on either side of his father, as well as Broken Hand and Red Cloud, riding for the first time as warriors. He could well imagine their pride and excitement.

He watched the riders until they were tiny dots on the horizon, then scanned the vast region of rolling green hills dotted with bushes and trees and brightly-colored wildflowers. Small rippling streams ran through the hills, reflecting the burning sun.

He turned and saw his young brother-in-law. Curly was looking toward the spot where the band of Sioux buffalo hunters had just disappeared.

"Fire Eagle, when will my father believe I am old enough to go on a buffalo hunt? Red Cloud and Broken Hand are only four grasses older than I am."

Fire Eagle laid a hand on Curly's shoulder and glanced toward the boy's teepee. Curly's father, medicine man Laughing Horse, sat inside, chanting over a fire. His high-pitched tones could be heard all over the village.

"Curly," Fire Eagle said, "speak English. The white teacher told us before he died that to talk with the white-eyes invaders, we must speak their language. We must use it among ourselves every day, so that we learn it as well as we know our own language."

"But why should we want to talk with the greedy white eyes, Fire Eagle? We must kill them, not talk with them."

"It is easier to speak of killing than to do the killing. They come in great numbers to our land, with weapons better than ours. To reason with them, our leaders must speak their language."

"But we have great warriors in Sioux nation," Curly said. "If we fight hard, we can drive the evil ones back to where they came from, or bury them."

Fire Eagle nodded, deep lines creasing his brow. "Your English has improved, Curly. Yes, I agree they should be killed for trespassing our land and trying to steal it, but since our people have mortal enemies among the Crow, Shoshone, and Pawnee, we must not war with the soldier coats as long as we can keep peace. Do you understand?"

"You mean, the soldier coats could weaken us so that our Indian enemies destroy us."

"Yes. We will only battle the whites if they try to steal our land."

"Then I understand. But when will my father see that I am old enough to go on the buffalo hunt? Other Oglala boys have gone, even when they were thirteen grasses, as I am."

Fire Eagle picked his words carefully. "Look around you, Curly. Our village is eight hundred strong. Nearly three hundred are warriors. Even most of the warriors have chosen to stay here today. There are some sixty boys who are between thirteen and eighteen grasses, but only Red Cloud and Broken Hand have chosen to go on this hunt."

"I would have chosen to go if my father had allowed it."

Fire Eagle sighed. "All right, I will tell you what Laughing Horse has said to me."

"Yes?"

"Your father says you have not shown the maturity an Oglala youth should have to be a buffalo hunter. You often question his decisions and commands like a small child. I also have noticed this, and so has your sister, Gentle Fawn. You must obey your father when he speaks, and not pout like a child when his decisions are different than your wishes. Curly has a strong will, but Curly must learn to obey his father in all things. Until he does, he will not be part of a buffalo hunt."

Curly's sour look disappeared. "I will do as you say, Fire Eagle. You are the greatest brother-in-law. Thank you." After a pause, he said, "Why did not Fire Eagle go on hunt today?"

Fire Eagle indicated the other warriors in the village. "We all have other things to do. Gray Shadow and those with him will do well and bring home plenty skinned-out buffalo."

Curly persisted. "Fire Eagle did not go on hunt because of my sister."

Fire Eagle smiled and looked toward his teepee. "It is best that I stay with Gentle Fawn. There are few moons left before our papoose comes."

At that moment, some of the village boys ran by, calling for Curly to join them. He took his leave of Fire Eagle and dashed off.

Fire Eagle ducked inside his teepee and sat down beside Gentle Fawn. She was in the last stages of pregnancy and lay on a crude pallet. Her mother, White Wing, tended her.

White Wing, who would soon be forty grasses, had a few silver strands in her black hair, and the crow's feet at the corners of her eyes were etching deeper. She was still pleasant to look upon, Fire Eagle thought. She and Gentle Fawn closely resembled each other.

"How is the pain in your back?" Fire Eagle said, as he took Gentle Fawn's hand.

"The same as for several days." Gentle Fawn forced a smile. "It will be worth it when our child is born."

Fire Eagle looked at his mother-in-law. "The back pain does not mean there is something wrong?"

"No, Fire Eagle. This is to be expected when she is heavy with child and the time draws near to give birth. Gentle Fawn is now maybe thirty moons from bringing your child into the world."

White Wing had delivered many babies, and Fire Eagle took comfort in her words.

She then said, "Gentle Fawn, like myself, has hip bones that are very close together. Because of this, I had trouble delivering her and Curly. I have been preparing Gentle Fawn for the difficult birth that is coming. But I came through it, and so will Gentle Fawn and your child."

Fire Eagle squeezed Gentle Fawn's hand and said softly, "I will be with you when the time comes to deliver our child. Wakan Tanka will be watching over you, and with White Wing to help, I know you and our child will be fine."

CHAPTER

TWO

C hief Gray Shadow's Oglala Sioux village of two hundred teepees was situated a mile off the road and almost exactly halfway between Fort Clark and a small white settlement called Point Nemaha. The fort and the white settlement were twenty miles apart.

Colonel Norvel Lawson, Fort Clark's commandant, commanded nearly two hundred men. Lawson was a West Point graduate, as were his five officers, Major Theron Tyler, Captain Lamar Dutton, Lieutenant Wylie Odoms, Lieutenant Frank Thompson, and Lieutenant William Dolan.

Tyler and Dutton, along with fifty-five men of the U.S. Fifth Infantry, had preceded their unit leader, Lieutenant Colonel George M. Brooke, to the fort by three months. Brooke was now on his way from Fort Dillard, Illinois, with the rest of the Fifth.

There was another contingent at the fort—the First U.S. Dragoons out of Jefferson City, Missouri. Lieutenants Wylie Odoms and William Dolan were part of this group and had arrived at Fort Clark four months previously with twenty-nine troopers.

Lieutenant Thompson hailed Major Tyler near the flagstaff, and Tyler waited as the lieutenant walked toward him. "You must be getting excited, sir," Thompson said. "Mrs. Tyler coming and all."

"That I am."

"Are you worried about her traveling in the army wagon train, sir?"

"You mean because of Indians or because she's about to deliver our child?"

"I was thinking of the latter, sir."

"Well, I really didn't want Andrea to make the trip, especially since it's our first child. But if she didn't come with Brooke, it could be months, or even a year or more, before another army unit from Illinois came this way."

Thompson shook his head. "I'm sure glad my Melinda's here, I'll tell you that. Brooke is scheduled to be here on June 25, isn't he?"

"That's right. I told Andrea I'd ride to Port Nemaha and meet her, since that's where they'll turn north off the beaten trail."

Thompson noticed Corporal Eddie Blaine heading their way from the colonel's quarters. Blaine stopped and saluted. "Major Tyler, sir, Colonel Lawson would like to see you in his office immediately."

"All right. Thank you. Well, Lieutenant, I'll see you later."

Tyler stepped inside the colonel's outer office and waited to be announced, then proceeded through the inner door and removed his campaign hat.

The fifty-year-old commandant had just swatted a fly and now swept it into the wastebasket with a rolled newspaper before looking up. "Sit down, Major."

Tyler eased onto a hardbacked chair and waited for the colonel to speak. Lawson leaned back, toying with his graying handlebar mustache. "I assume you know there were three buffalo hunters in here to see me."

"Yes, sir. I was told about them right after they entered your office. And...I can still smell them."

"Not the cleanest bunch, are they?" Lawson said with a chuckle.

"Well, sir, I suppose they bathe once a decade, whether they need it or not."

The colonel chuckled again. "They gave me some valuable information. They've just returned from up north. Thought I should know that the Sioux have set up camp in the last few days some twenty-five miles north of here."

"I see. Did they have any idea what band of Sioux?"

"One of the hunters said it's a Hunkpapa band, and their new chief, Sitting Bull, is with them."

"Just warriors?"

"No. Women and children, too. Even some ex-warriors too old to fight."

"How many are in the camp?"

"The hunters weren't sure. The Sioux were just beginning to set up their teepees when they passed by."

"I guess the best thing is to take a patrol up there and see what we can find out. I'll put together some men and—"

"No need for you to go." Lawson glanced at another pesky fly buzzing in the window. "I want you to send Lieutenant Dolan and his dragoon unit. Twenty-seven men and Dolan ought to be enough."

Lawson noticed Tyler's slight frown. "Something wrong, Major?"

"Oh, ah…no, sir. I don't think any of the Indians would attack a scouting unit of that size."

"All right then. If you'll inform Lieutenant Dolan right away, he can make preparations this afternoon. They can ride out at sunup."

Tyler rose from the chair. "I'll deliver the order, sir."

——◆——

At sunrise the scouting patrol saddled up. Major Tyler moved up beside Lieutenant Dolan as he swung into the saddle. Dolan was perhaps a year or two older than Tyler, and it didn't sit well that the younger man outranked him. Most of the time Dolan's lips turned down, and his forehead seemed to have a built-in scowl.

"I want to remind you, Lieutenant," Tyler said, "that Colonel Lawson is emphatic that you understand this mission. By no means are you to launch an offensive on the Hunkpapas. You are simply to determine how many of them are in the camp...especially warriors. Understand?"

"I understand...sir."

Dolan wheeled his horse around, barked a command for his men to rein into formation, and led them toward the gate. As the sentries swung the gate wide, Dolan looked over his shoulder, a expression of deep resentment in his eyes.

Lieutenant Thompson had moved up beside Major Tyler to watch the dragoons leave. "Sir, I understand you have some misgivings about Lieutenant Dolan."

"Oh?"

"Yes, sir. Scuttlebutt. Must be so, the way he looked at you."

Tyler was silent for a moment, then said, "I've been here for three months, Lieutenant, and I've seen enough to know he's a hothead. From what I'm able to pick up from his men, I think he's been killing Indians on the sly."

"You say his men told you this, sir?"

"No. What I've learned wasn't meant for my ears...or for those of any other officer. When I questioned the men in private, they just said I misunderstood what I heard. Call it a gut feeling, but I think Dolan's men are covering for him."

"Have you discussed this with Colonel Lawson?"

"No. I have no proof. I'll have to wait till I can prove Dolan's guilt before I go to the colonel."

"That's wise, sir. You may have picked up that Colonel Lawson puts a lot of stock in Lieutenant Dolan."

Two hours after riding out of Fort Clark, Lt. William Dolan and his scouting party dropped into a shallow draw and climbed to the opposite side. As they got near the crest, Dolan raised a hand, signaling the men to pull rein.

Sergeant Leonard Cahill rode next to Dolan. "It's the Hunkpapa camp, all right, sir."

Dolan turned in the saddle to speak to his patrol. "The Sioux camp is off to our right about five hundred yards in a thin stand of trees. Some fifty yards to our left is a grassy mound about thirty feet high. We'll swing around on the west side of it and stash the horses. Then we'll climb up on the mound and take a good look."

The men dismounted, and with their new short-barreled Henry .44 rifles in hand, they crawled up the mound and spread out, lying flat. To the east, thin columns of smoke floated skyward from a half-dozen fires among the teepees.

Lieutenant Dolan studied the camp through binoculars for a long moment, then said, "I can't see any warriors or ponies down there. They're probably out huntin' buffalo or other game, or scoutin' to see if there are any of us blue coats around. All I can make out are women and children. Maybe two or three old men."

"Kind of hard to get a good count from here, Lieutenant," Jared Holloman said. "Looks to be better than sixty, I'd say."

Dolan peered through the binoculars, silently moving his lips. "I count seventy-four teepees, Holloman."

Sergeant Cahill did a quick calculation. "That'd make somewhere around three hundred of 'em, sir, figurin' four redskins to a teepee. That's what it averages out, doesn't it?"

"Yeah," Dolan said. "Allowin' for a few of the old men and

their squaws a teepee each, there have to be about seventy warriors."

He lifted the binoculars for another look. "We'll just ride through the camp, shoot as many as we can in one sweep, then head back for the fort."

Sergeant Cahill exchanged glances with Holloman. "Lieutenant, sir, the rest of us have been talkin' about this killin' of Indian women, children, and old men. We'd just rather not do it anymore."

Dolan set hard eyes on his sergeant. "What're you talkin' about, you don't want to kill Indians anymore?"

Cahill swallowed hard and met the lieutenant's gaze. "Sir, one of these times Colonel Lawson's going to find out and have our hides. So far, we've stayed out of trouble 'cause he was under the impression that those we needlessly killed were victims of a battle with the warriors in camp."

"Needlessly? *Needlessly?* Sergeant, it has never been needless to kill redskinned savages! So it bothers you to kill the old men, does it?"

Cahill's lips quivered. "Well, sir—"

"Those old men used to be warriors. In case you've forgotten, they killed white people! Do you understand that? They slaughtered white people who came through here twenty, thirty years ago! They deserve to die!"

"But, sir," another man spoke up, "I'm to the point I can hardly sleep. I close my eyes at night and picture the little children and women. I—"

"What's the matter...you got part of you're brain missin'? Those little Indian boys will grow up to be warriors, and they'll kill white people! The younger women will give birth to more boys and they'll eventually become warriors who'll kill white people! The little girls will grow up and give birth to even more of 'em, who'll kill white people! The baby boys the old women produced are now the wicked-eyed savages we have to kill, because if we don't, they'll kill us and our kind!"

"But, sir, we're taking the lives of those who can't even defend themselves. That's nothing short of murder!"

"Murder? It's execution! We're executin' the old men for their guilt in already killin' whites, and the rest of 'em for the deaths of whites they'll bring about if we don't execute 'em!"

"Sir," Holloman said, "I don't know you as well as these other men do. May I ask you something?"

"What is it?" Dolan's scowl lines deepened.

"Well, sir, you seem to hate the Indians in a way the rest of us don't. Is there a reason for that?"

Dolan's face seemed to swell as emotion darkened it. "Yeah, Holloman, there's a reason, all right. When I was nine years old back in Ohio, some dirty sneakin' Shawnees crept onto our farm and killed my parents, my brother, and two sisters. If I'd been at the house when they came, they'd have killed me too. I was just comin' back from a friend's farm when I saw the filthy devils ridin' away. I hid till they were out of sight, then ran to the house. If you'd seen what I did, you'd hate the savages too." Dolan fixed Holloman with fiery eyes. "Now, don't even think of givin' me the old, 'Well, those were Shawnees, Lieutenant; these are Sioux.' An Indian is an Indian, and as far as I'm concerned, the only good Indian is a dead one!"

For a moment the only sound was that of the soft breeze that plucked at the men's hat brims and tufted the grass. "Now, white soldiers, you and I are goin' to mount up and ride into that stinkin' village. We're goin' to blast away at every redskin we see, no matter what gender or what age. And we're goin' to keep doin' it every time we get the chance."

He looked at the faces around him before adding, "And the guy who gets cold feet and rats on the rest of us will live to be sorry for blabbin'. He just won't live very long."

No one spoke.

"All right," Dolan said, "let's ride into that village and make some *good* Indians."

———•———

Sub-Chief Black Dog and thirty-one warriors were pleased with their hunting trip. They were returning to the Hunkpapa camp with seven deer.

Black Dog wondered if Chief Sitting Bull and the thirty-three warriors who had ridden the opposite direction had been as fortunate. They had all come from the main Hunkpapa village near the Nebraska-Wyoming border to hunt big game for a few weeks.

Black Dog was in his early fifties. He had shown some signs of losing his strength but was still considered a fierce warrior. His hatred for the white man had not abated in the slightest. He wore a sub-chief's rawhide headband with horsehair dyed red and woven to resemble lightning bolts.

Black Dog rode in the lead, flanked by his warrior sons. As they drew within a mile of camp and topped a rise, they saw the grassy mound covered with white soldiers.

Black Dog twisted around and commanded his warriors to prepare for battle. The blue coats were trespassing on Sioux territory and would now be punished.

Some of the Hunkpapa warriors carried muskets; others carried bows and arrows. Hammers were cocked and arrows notched to bowstrings as Black Dog raised his feathered musket, shook it defiantly, and with a loud guttural exclamation, released the Sioux war cry, *"Hokahey!"*

The warriors urged their mounts to a gallop, charging full speed at the white soldiers. Their earsplitting war cry turned into high-pitched, bloodcurdling whoops as they spread out in a wide formation, thundering toward the mound.

Lieutenant Dolan and his men were halfway down the slope when they heard the rumble of hooves and the Hunkpapas' war cry.

"Quick, men!" Dolan shouted. "Move around to the east side! That'll protect our horses! We'll have to fight from behind the boulders and grassy humps! Let's go!"

Dolan counted rapidly as the enemy spread out and swung around the south side of the mound, forming a giant corral, then turned toward the soldiers hunkering down on the east side. He noted that seven pintos were carrying two warriors. "There are just over thirty of 'em, men! We can take 'em! Hold your fire till I say!"

The Indians advanced within a hundred yards and began firing. Arrows thwacked into the sod behind the soldiers, and bullets thudded into soft earth or ricocheted off the boulders.

When the Hunkpapas came within fifty yards, Lieutenant Dolan bellowed, "Fire at will, men! Make every shot count! Have your knives ready! They'll be comin' in for hand-to-hand if we don't get 'em in the first two or three volleys!"

CHAPTER

THREE

———◆———

The warriors riding double hopped off, while the mounted Indians made a swift pass, shooting one soldier and losing two of their own. They regrouped and came in for another pass.

Dolan saw a soldier drop to his left but kept his eyes on a broad back and squeezed the trigger. The Indian rode away untouched. Dolan swore and fired at another Hunkpapa just as a bullet skinned the sod a few inches from his face, flinging dirt into his eyes. He ducked low, furiously blinking his eyes.

He was just getting his eyes cleared when the Indians charged again, and Jared Holloman grabbed his chest and fell backwards. Dolan could sense the fear around him.

"Keep firin', men! We can take 'em! Don't ease up! Let 'em have it!"

No sooner had he shouted encouragement than he saw wild-eyed warriors swarming in on foot.

Black Dog found the man with highest rank and bolted toward Dolan. One glance at the Indian's headband and Dolan knew it was the sub-chief. He aimed his revolver and squeezed the trigger, but the hammer clicked on a spent shell.

Black Dog dashed forward as Dolan grabbed the knife at his

AL LACY

belt and braced himself. The Indian drove his full weight into Dolan while skillfully avoiding the knife. Dolan managed to roll free, but when Black Dog lunged again, the two became locked in mortal combat.

William Dolan was a fierce fighter and exceptionally strong. Black Dog, killer of many a white man, found this one more than a worthy opponent. A sudden kick from Dolan sent Black Dog's knife sailing through the air, and the blue coat quickly straddled him. Black Dog struggled with everything in him to keep Dolan's hand from plunging the knife.

Dolan punched Black Dog with his free hand. The blow stunned Black Dog, yet he continued to struggle and managed to tighten his grasp on the white man's wrist.

It was not enough.

One of the Hunkpapa warriors saw Dolan plunge the knife into Black Dog's chest and turned to shout that their leader was dead. It took only seconds for the warriors to lose heart. The Hunkpapas dashed to their horses and galloped away.

"Don't let 'em get away!" Dolan shouted. "Load your guns and—" His eyes finally took in the scene. Eleven soldiers down, at least five of them dead. The rest looked half-dead, their uniforms torn and bloody.

Dolan swung a listless hand. "See to the wounded," he said. Then he picked up his revolver and moved about, examining the Indians who lay on the ground. Four dead, including Black Dog, and five wounded. He ordered two soldiers to drag the wounded Indians to one spot.

Dolan punched out spent shells and fed cartridges from his belt pouch into the cylinder. Sergeant Cahill moved up beside him. "Lieutenant! What are you doing?"

"Exterminatin' vermin, Lenny. Exterminatin' vermin."

"But, sir, this isn't proper military procedure! We don't execute wounded enemies!"

"I'm not leavin' for the fort with one savage still breathin',

26

Sergeant. Since when is military procedure necessary when you're exterminatin' vermin?"

"But, sir—"

"See to our wounded men like I told you, Sergeant!"

Cahill glanced at the helpless Indians. It seemed they knew what was coming.

The dragoons had overlooked Dolan's killing in the villages and camps, but somehow this seemed worse. They gazed in helpless horror as he snapped back the hammer and pointed the gun toward the ground.

It was almost noon when Lieutenant Dolan and his troops returned to Fort Clark. The dead were draped over the backs of their horses, and each wounded man rode double with a comrade.

Dolan felt vindicated to some degree. More Sioux dead than white men. Nine Indians...five soldiers.

As the solemn procession drew near the fort, the sentry on watch swung wide the gate and said, "Lieutenant Dolan, I'll run and tell Doc Fillmore we've got wounded men and that he should meet you at the infirmary as soon as possible."

"Right," Dolan said. "Find Colonel Lawson and tell him we had a run-in with the Hunkpapas. Five men dead, six wounded. I'll be at his office to make a report as soon as Doc Fillmore checks on the wounded."

"Yes, sir," the corporal said, and took off running.

Dr. Harley Fillmore rushed to the infirmary less than ten minutes later to find the wounded soldiers lying on cots. Colonel Lawson and Major Tyler were not far behind. The rest of Dolan's dragoons were gathered near the infirmary porch.

Colonel Lawson ran his gaze over the wounded men and said to Dolan, "The report can wait until we see what Doc says, Lieutenant. You can do that in my office."

"Yes, sir." Dolan glanced at Major Tyler then quickly looked away.

Other men began to gather at the porch of the infirmary as word of Dolan's battle spread.

Thirty minutes later, Colonel Lawson emerged with Tyler and Dolan.

"How does it look, Colonel?" one of the troopers asked. "They going to make it?"

"Dr. Fillmore says none of them are in danger of dying. He's got some bullets to dig out and some surgery to do, but they'll be all right in time."

"What happened, Colonel?" asked another trooper.

"Lieutenant Dolan hasn't had an opportunity to make his report yet. So I don't know much more than you do."

The three officers crossed the parade ground to the colonel's office. Dolan didn't like having Tyler present, but Tyler was second in command at the fort, and it was out of Dolan's control.

"All right, Lieutenant Dolan," the colonel said, "tell us what happened."

Dolan said he and his men had crawled the mound on their bellies and studied the Hunkpapa camp. He could see no warriors or horses, so he thought Sitting Bull and his men were out hunting or scouting. He counted seventy-four teepees, which told him there were approximately seventy warriors and three hundred Indians in the camp.

Dolan told how the Hunkpapas bore down on them as they were descending the mound to return to the fort. He and his men couldn't avoid the fight. He'd killed Black Dog in a hand-to-hand knife fight and the other Hunkpapas had run away.

Major Tyler had been a soldier all his adult life, and he knew how to read them. When he'd first seen the pallid faces of the dragoons as they stood outside the infirmary, he sensed that something more was wrong than that five of their friends had been killed and six lay wounded. Now he turned on his chair to look at

Dolan "You haven't told us about Indian casualties in this battle, Lieutenant. How many did you and your men kill? How many wounded were there?"

"Nine dead, sir. No wounded."

"No wounded?"

"No, sir, they all fought to the death."

Tyler shook his head slowly. "I fought a lot of battles in the Mexican War, but I never saw one with no wounded."

"Are you questioning my veracity, Major?"

"Either that or your eyesight. Maybe you didn't check all nine closely. Maybe some were still alive."

A flush brightened Dolan's cheeks. "Colonel, I object! The major's calling me a liar!"

Colonel Lawson looked a bit confused and said, "Major, I wish you'd be a bit more lenient here. This man is a fellow officer."

Tyler tried to keep his voice under control. "Colonel, let's bring in Sergeant Cahill and two or three men of his choice. Let's see what they tell us about this incident."

Lawson cocked his head. "Major Tyler, I realize it's quite rare to have a battle of any kind with no wounded survivors, but why do you question Lieutenant Dolan's word?"

"Because the dragoons have six wounded. How could a battle like this produce a half-dozen wounded men on one side and none on the other? I could believe it if there had been only nine of them fighting Lieutenant Dolan's entire force. But from what he told us, there were at least as many Indians as there were soldiers."

"Just what are you getting at, Major?"

"I've heard conversations around this fort ever since I arrived here, sir, that lead me to believe Lieutenant Dolan has a deep-seated hatred for Indians and might sometimes let that hatred override his good judgment. To put it bluntly, sir, I'm wondering if the wounded Sioux in this morning's battle were executed."

Dolan features contorted with rage. "I'll show you, Tyler! Colonel, I demand you bring Sergeant Cahill here right now! And any other of my men that you choose!"

Without a word, Lawson left his chair and stepped into the next room to instruct his aide.

Soon Cahill and the others stood before the officers. Colonel Lawson questioned them, as did Major Tyler. They performed exactly as Dolan knew they would. When the interview was over and the men had been dismissed, Colonel Lawson rose to his feet.

"Well, Major Tyler, are you satisfied now?"

"No, sir."

Lawson blinked. "Why not?"

"Those men were under duress, sir. Certainly you could see that."

"They've just lost five of their friends, Major. How do you expect them to act?"

"There's a difference between grief and duress, sir, but nothing more can be done now. Testimony has been given."

"Very well. Lieutenant Dolan, I will expect your written report on my desk first thing tomorrow morning."

"Yes, sir." Dolan nodded stiffly, trying hard to suppress his wrath. "May I be excused?"

"You are excused. And so are you, Major."

Lawson stood in the doorway of the outer office for a long moment, watching the two officers walk away in opposite directions.

From the desk behind him, the corporal who served as his aide said, "Were you able to solve whatever problem you were handling, sir?"

Lawson waited until both men had passed from view before answering. Then he said, "No, I don't think so."

That night, Dolan left his quarters just as the enlisted men were bedding down. He crossed the parade ground under a star-studded sky and moved toward the small shed behind the infirmary. The bodies of the men to be buried the next morning were lying there in a row. Each body was covered with a blanket, and a low-burning lantern cast a dim light, forming deep shadows in the corners of the room.

Dolan removed his hat and turned it round and round with trembling fingers. A hot ball of wrath burned in his chest as he said aloud, "You men rest in peace. Your lieutenant will get even with those stinkin' Hunkpapas for killin' you. That's a promise."

Dolan stayed with his dead men for a while, then donned his hat and stepped outside. A tall form detached itself from the shadows, causing Dolan to start. "Oh, it's *you*. What do you want?"

"Just to talk to you a minute."

"Well, make it quick. I'm headin' for bed."

The brim of Tyler's campaign hat hid his expression. "I'll overlook your insolence toward an officer of higher rank, Lieutenant, but if I ever learn that wounded Sioux were executed out there today, I'll not overlook *that*. Got it?"

"Colonel Lawson's satisfied. Why aren't you?"

"Just call it a soldier's intuition, Lieutenant. Good night." With that, Tyler turned and walked away.

Lieutenants William Dolan and Wylie Odoms shared the same officers' quarters. When Dolan stepped inside, Odoms looked up from the book he'd been reading. "Feeling better now?" he asked.

"Maybe a little."

"Guess I should've insisted on going with you this morning, Bill," Odoms said.

"You had work to do here. Besides, if you'd gone along, *you* might be one of those poor men lyin' dead in that shed." Dolan plunked himself down on an overstuffed horsehair sofa and gazed at his friend. "Wylie, you know about that Sioux custom with the scaffolds when someone dies…"

Odoms bent the corner of the page and closed the book. "Yeah. They believe the spirit stays in the body for seven days after death, and if they're buried before the seven days are up, the spirit of the dead person remains in the ground forever. So…what are you thinking?"

"Any Sioux will tell you the worst tragedy that could happen to them is to be imprisoned in the ground forever."

"Don't tell me you're going to mess with some Indian corpses."

"Precisely."

"Bill, you're out of your mind."

"Yes. I'm out of my mind with fury and the desire to avenge my men!"

"And just how do you plan to do that?"

"I'm goin' to sneak into that Hunkpapa camp four nights from now, steal the body of Black Dog, and bury it. I'll wait a week, then see that a map gets into the hands of ol' Sitting Bull, showin' him where the body is buried and declarin' it was buried the same night it was stolen." Dolan threw back his head and laughed. "That'll get to 'em! They'll mourn for ol' Black Dog's spirit forever!"

Odoms rose to his feet and stood beside Dolan. "And just how do you plan to sneak into that Hunkpapa stronghold and snatch the body?"

"Well, their mourning ceremonies will only last through tonight and the next two nights. On the fourth night, I'll sneak in there and stampede their horses. While they're chasin' after their animals, I'll snatch Black Dog's corpse."

Odoms looked skeptical. "You'll never get away with it, Bill.

There's no way you can pull that off."

A slow grin spread over Dolan's face. "Didn't I tell you? I meant *we*. *We* will sneak in there, stampede the horses, and snatch Black Dog's body."

Odoms backed away, shaking his head. "No, Bill. It's too dangerous. I don't want any part of it."

"Now, hold on, ol' pal. Have you forgotten that I saved your worthless hide back in February when we fought those yappin' Cheyennes over at Dove Creek? I mean, *saved* it at the risk of my own?"

Odoms looked at the floor. "No, I haven't forgotten."

"Well, then," Dolan said with a hollow laugh, "it seems you owe me, don't you?"

Wylie paused a long time and then nodded. "Yeah. I guess I owe you."

FOUR

n the fourth night after the Hunkpapa Sioux warriors were killed at the grassy mound, sixty-two solemn-faced warriors sat around a large fire in the center of camp. Five of them were old men who had not fought for many years.

Seven young warriors were gathered nearby under the cottonwood trees, ready to beat their drums—hollowed-out logs covered with tightly stretched buffalo hide.

The women and children looked on from the fringes. Small fires burned behind them amongst the trees, where a feast of venison was cooking. The Hunkpapas had not eaten since the day the nine warriors had been killed. Tonight they would break their fast.

Sitting Bull, who was still in his teepee, had grieved especially hard over the loss of Black Dog. Now that the time of mourning was almost over, the Indians would eat the feast of "New Life" and attempt to resume life as it was before their beloved warriors were killed.

At the northern edge of camp, the half-moon and the light of several fires revealed nine gaunt scaffolds. The night wind sighed through the cottonwoods and made the poles creak and whipped the old red blankets covering the bodies.

There was an open space in the circle of men reserved for

their honored chief. Next to that spot, medicine man Big Buffalo sat cross-legged, wearing a buffalo horn headdress. His high-pitched chant filled the night air as he shook his bone rattles and committed the spirits of the dead warriors to Wakan Tanka, the Sky Father. When three more nights had passed, their spirits would walk away and begin the long journey to Wanagi Yata, the home of the Sky People.

The women and children with a view of the chief's teepee watched the closed flap. The moment Sitting Bull left the teepee and took his place among the warriors, the time of mourning would be officially over and the feast of New Life would begin.

Big Buffalo's chanting stopped and silence prevailed. The only sound was the low moan of the wind through the treetops. Then the drums broke the silence with a throbbing, measured cadence. Seconds later, the stalwart Hunkpapa chief, a lean figure in his late thirties, emerged from his teepee. Sitting Bull's brilliance as a battle strategist had made him one of the youngest chiefs in the Sioux nation.

The warriors at the perimeter of the circle started to chant, and the squaws joined in with a shrill keening.

Sitting Bull wore the full eagle-feathered war bonnet of a Lakota chief. Draped over his left arm was a section of a white buffalo's hide, which Black Dog had killed a short time earlier. The inside of the hide had been scraped smooth and was covered with sacred paintings. In his right hand he carried a long feathered lance.

He walked slowly toward the circle of warriors and came to a halt at the place next to Big Buffalo. Suddenly he drove the sharp tip of the lance into the ground and all chanting and keening stopped, and the throbbing of the drums quickly faded to silence.

Sitting Bull raised both hands toward the night sky, fingers stretched out, and uttered a primal cry to the Sky Father, then spoke in his deep guttural voice. "Hear your chief, O Hunkpapas.

We now enter the time of New Life for our people. The spirits of our brave warriors will soon journey to the Sky Father, and we must return to the raising of our children and the preserving of our land from the hands of our enemies. Let the feast begin."

The Hunkpapas ate heartily for over an hour, then certain warriors joined in a fire dance. Late in the evening, they began putting out the small fires, preparing to retire for the night. The large fire was allowed to burn, but no more fuel was added, and slowly it dwindled.

When Sitting Bull entered his teepee for the night, the rest of the people did the same, except for four sentries positioned at strategic spots on the edge of camp. A young warrior named Spotted Coyote was assigned to the area around the rope corral near the death scaffolds.

Spotted Coyote slowly paced as the night deepened. Soon the fire in the center of the camp had burned down to glowing red embers.

Sitting Bull was just drifting off to sleep when he heard a horse's shrill neigh. It continued, and then came the sound of pounding hooves.

He sat up, blinking against the darkness. His ears told him the horses were out of the corral, the sound of their thundering hooves beginning to fade in the distance.

As Sitting Bull stepped out of the teepee, he saw warriors dashing about, calling to each other. Lame Elk and Two White Feathers ran up to tell him something had spooked the horses. They had jumped the single rope and run away.

Sitting Bull frowned, not yet fully understanding. "Where is Spotted Coyote? He is responsible for guarding the horses."

"We did not see him," Lame Elk said.

Puffy clouds drifted over the half-moon as Sitting Bull and

the other warriors hurried toward the rope corral. A quick search did not locate Spotted Coyote. The warriors gathered around their chief.

Sitting Bull commanded all the warriors to go after the horses, then made his way back to his teepee. He wondered if his Crow, Shoshone, or Pawnee enemies had seized Spotted Coyote and frightened the ponies into running away. When daylight came, he would study the ground around the camp and find some answers.

The moon had reached its zenith and had started its downward arc toward the west when the warriors returned with the horses three hours later and ran them inside the rope corral. Sitting Bull was waiting for them.

"Did you find all of the horses?"

"Yes," said the closest warrior.

"Good. We will use what is left of the night to rest, then search for Spotted Coyote in daylight. We will also study the ground to see if we can tell who did this."

Sitting Bull waited until his warriors had scattered to their teepees before returning to his own. He glanced toward Black Dog's scaffold and halted in his tracks.

Sitting Bull's heart started to pound as he rushed to the scaffold. All that remained were the rawhide thongs that lashed the platform to the upright poles and the shrunken intestine of a buffalo stuffed with pemmican to sustain Black Dog's spirit on his long journey to Wanagi Yata.

An enormous rage welled up in Sitting Bull. Now he knew what the stampeding was about. He threw back his head and let out a primal cry. He repeated it over and over until his warriors came running. His blazing eyes roamed over their dark, moon-touched faces, waiting for them to realize the scaffold no longer held Black Dog's corpse.

Sitting Bull's fiery anger was contagious as emotions flared and some asked the chief what he was going to do.

Sitting Bull said they would have to wait for daylight to

inspect the ground. It could have been the hated Crows, Shoshones, or Pawnees...or it could have been wicked white men. Either way, they had stolen Black Dog's body and had taken Spotted Coyote.

At dawn, Chief Sitting Bull was just rising from his straw bed when an excited voice called to him. The chief threw back the tent flap to find Lame Elk, Two White Feathers, and a third warrior named Little Mountain holding dead diamondback rattlers.

"What is this?"

"We found them in the rope corral at first light," Two White Feathers said. "Some of the horses are sick. Our enemies who stole Black Dog's body threw the snakes into the corral, knowing they would strike the horses and stampede them. The snakes died under the hooves. We can tell that at least four of the horses have been bitten."

Near the corral and scaffold they found indistinct footprints leading to the creek that ran past the camp. There were no other signs. Apparently the intruders had ridden their horses for several miles in the middle of the creek, coming and going.

Four more days passed. At sunrise on the ninth morning, Sitting Bull was just coming out of his teepee when Lame Elk and Little Mountain dashed up. Lame Elk held out an empty brown paper bag. "We found this paper stuck on the low limb of a tree at the edge of camp!" he said.

Sitting Bull accepted the flattened bag and studied the markings on it. It was a crude map with an X by the north shore of Soda Lake, which was identified in English. Sitting Bull knew English well. Black Dog's name was written by the X.

The chief mounted his pinto and led a band of warriors toward Soda Lake, six or seven miles to the northeast. When they arrived on the north shore they could see a mound rising more than a foot above ground level.

The Hunkpapas eyed each other uneasily. Long Man, a subchief, dismounted first and picked up another brown paper bag weighted by a rock at the head of the grave. He read it silently and handed it to Sitting Bull.

Sitting Bull read the note and handed it back to Long Man. Then he dismounted and stood over the grave, clenching his fists and grinding his teeth in anger and helpless anguish.

Long Man read the words to the other warriors:

Sitting Bull—This grave was filled the very night we stole the body.

The warriors' blood ran cold. They began clawing at the soft mound of dirt while their chief looked on, his face showing the depth of his grief. Long Man and Two White Feathers lifted Black Dog's dirt-caked body from its shallow grave, then froze in disbelief.

"Chief, we have found Spotted Coyote too."

The sight of the young warrior's body beneath that of Black Dog's was more than the chief could take. He trembled at the thought that both spirits would be locked in the ground forever. He lifted his hands toward the sky, and a piteous wail burst from his lips and echoed across the sunlit waters of Soda Lake.

When Sitting Bull and his warriors arrived back at the camp with the bodies, the Hunkpapas wailed uncontrollably.

The bodies were buried for the final time in separate graves, and Chief Sitting Bull stood amongst his men, choking on the lump in his throat. He was confident the messages on the brown paper bags had come from white men. He suspected that the guilty parties were part of the army patrol that had killed Black Dog and the eight other warriors.

His mind went back to that day. He and his hunting party had returned to the camp at sunset after they had retrieved the warriors' bodies. The surviving warriors had explained they had left the fight when they saw Black Dog die. They knew there were five wounded warriors, as well as four dead. When they went back after the soldier coats had left, all nine were dead.

Sitting Bull decided to ride to Fort Clark under a white flag and discuss the incident with the soldier-coat chief. He would also tell him about the stampeding of the horses, the theft of Black Dog's body, the murder of Spotted Coyote, and the sacrilege of burying them too soon.

Colonel Lawson and two dozen troopers had ridden out of Fort Clark at sunrise for a four-day jaunt to Fort Laramie, Wyoming.

At ten o'clock, two dragoon troopers were just leaving Major Tyler's office the back way when there was a knock on the front door. Tyler waited until the troopers were gone and then called, "The door's open!"

A corporal, whom Tyler recognized as one of the sentries at the gate, appeared. "Major, sir..."

"Yes, Corporal Ballard?"

"I...uh...well, we've got the big Hunkpapa himself at the gate."

Tyler's eyes widened. "You mean, Sitting Bull?"

"Yes, sir. He's got three braves with him. They're carrying a white flag. Sitting Bull says he wants a parley with the soldier-coat chief. I explained that Colonel Lawson is gone and told him you're in charge. He wants to see you."

Tyler took his hat from a peg. "All right. Let's go see what he wants."

The major was taller and longer-legged than the corporal, and Ballard had to double-time it to keep up. When they reached the gate, another sentry was holding it partially open.

Word had spread fast that Sitting Bull was at the gate, and

small groups of soldiers stood about the compound, gawking at the visitors.

Tyler was instantly impressed with the chief's aura of dignity. The morning breeze toyed with the colorful feathers of his full headdress and fluttered the white flag on a pole held by one of the braves.

"Chief Sitting Bull, I am Major Theron Tyler. I believe Corporal Ballard explained that our commandant is not here, and that I am in charge in his stead."

Sitting Bull nodded slowly. "He told me. I am asking for parley with you."

"Certainly. Please dismount and come with me to my office. What about your braves? Do you want them to come with you?"

"They may remain here." Sitting Bull slid from the pinto and handed his musket to the nearest brave. He then turned toward the major and did a half-bow, touching the fingertips of his left hand to his forehead, the Lakota sign of deepest respect.

Tyler knew the custom and did the same, then gestured toward the fort's interior. "Come, Chief Sitting Bull. I welcome you."

As the two men walked across the parade ground, almost every eye in the fort watched their progress.

A nervous Wylie Odoms put his head close to William Dolan and said in a low tone, "The big Hunkpapa's got to be here because of what we did."

Dolan chuckled. "Sitting Bull can't prove a thing."

Tyler pushed open his office door and gestured for the chief to enter. Rather than sitting behind his desk, he positioned two chairs in front so that they faced each other.

"Now, Chief, what did you want to talk to me about?"

"Major Tyler, we are enemies because the white man has

come to our land, interrupted our way of life, killed our buffalo by the hundreds, and laid hands on much of our property. You understand, then, that we fight you, even as you would fight us if we invaded your land."

"I assure you that I understand, Chief," Tyler said. "Most white people who head west are not interested in settling on your land. They simply want to pass through it without being attacked. Because of hostilities on the part of your tribe and so many others, we have built these forts and manned them for the protection of our people. Do you understand that?"

Sitting Bull nodded. "If this were always so—that they would pass through and not shoot our buffalo or corrupt our land, and not decide to settle on and steal land from us—there would not be bloodshed, Major."

"Believe me, Chief, that's the way I'd like to see it. Maybe someday it will be that way. Now, you wanted to talk to me about something."

Sitting Bull told the major everything that had happened, from the battle on the grassy mound to the sacrilegious burial of two warriors' bodies at Soda Lake.

A slow boil spread through Major Theron Tyler. What he'd just learned from the two troopers who'd slipped out the back door and now from Sitting Bull confirmed that Lieutenant Dolan had indeed executed the wounded Hunkpapa warriors. Probably he was also the instigator of the theft of Black Dog's body and the murder of Spotted Coyote.

Tyler took a deep breath and let it out slowly. "Chief, you said awhile ago that we are enemies. I'm sorry for that, but you're right. We both know that the killing of warriors and soldiers is a natural part of warfare. But I know we both agree that wounded men should not be murdered in cold blood."

Sitting Bull's face remained impassive. "You are correct, Major Tyler. And Sitting Bull is very disturbed by what your men did to his wounded warriors at the grassy mound. He is even more disturbed by the sacrilege to Black Dog's body and the murder and burial of Spotted Coyote."

"Chief, I disagree with your belief that a man's spirit must remain in the ground forever if he is buried within seven days after death. But I want you to know that I am sincerely sorry for what was done to Black Dog and Spotted Coyote. It may have been someone in this fort who did the sacrilege, but certainly they are not going to admit it, and I have no way of proving who did it."

Sitting Bull stiffened. "Sitting Bull wants revenge for the deeds!"

"I can't blame you, Chief. But I must make it clear that even if I could prove it was men of this fort who committed the sacrilege, they would be punished army-style, not by Sitting Bull."

"Major Tyler, do I have your word that the men who executed my wounded warriors will be disciplined severely by you and your soldier-coat chief?"

"If I can prove who did it, that person or persons will be disciplined, Chief Sitting Bull. You have my word on it."

"And if it can be proven who committed the sacrilege, will they be severely disciplined?"

"Yes, sir. You have my word on that, too."

The chief rose to his feet. "Then Sitting Bull will go now."

Tyler walked the Hunkpapa leader to the gate and bid him farewell. He then made a beeline for Lieutenant Dolan, whom he had seen at the toolshed with Lieutenant Odoms. The two were just moving away as Tyler approached. "Hold on, Dolan. I want to talk to you."

Wylie Odoms's heart leaped to his throat and seemed to freeze there. He felt only slight relief when the major called only Dolan to his office.

Dolan remained cool and met Tyler's eyes without flinching after hearing the accusation. "So they each had two bullets in 'em. What does that prove? I'm tellin' you now, as I told you before, all nine of those redskins fought to the death."

"You're a liar, Dolan! I just got a visit from two of your troopers. They told me you executed those warriors in spite of Sergeant Cahill's pleading with you not to do it."

Dolan's face darkened. "That's a stinkin' lie! I want to know who said that!"

"Request denied." Tyler then told Dolan what Sitting Bull had said about the burial of his two warriors. "I want to know who helped you do that, Dolan."

"What? You think *I* did that? What kind of fool would sneak into that camp of savages to steal a body?"

"The kind of fool I'm looking at right now. Of course, I can't prove it was you, Lieutenant, so I can't discipline you by army authority."

Dolan chuckled. "Yeah? Well, you don't have any proof that I executed those warriors, either, Major Theron Tyler, *sir.* It's my word against the word of those troopers."

"You're right. It's your word against theirs. I can't discipline you by military authority, but I *can* discipline you in private behind the barracks."

Dolan's brow puckered. "You mean…a bare-knuckle fight?"

"Exactly."

"You mean that *you,* a major, would strike *me,* a lowly lieutenant?"

"We'll remove our coats and rank insignias. This will be just between you and me, man to man. I'll make sure Colonel Lawson understands that's the way it was."

Dolan was grinning now. "Well, this is my red-letter day, Theron," he said, as he slipped out of his coat. "I've wanted to beat the daylights out of you ever since you first showed up at this fort. It'll be a pleasure to pound you to a bloody pulp."

CHAPTER
FIVE

As soon as Tyler and Dolan stepped outside, Tyler spied just the man he was looking for, talking to Sergeant Jake Finch, the blacksmith.

"Lieutenant!"

Frank Thompson turned around at hearing Tyler's voice. "Yes, Major?"

"See you a minute?"

Thompson said a few more words to Finch, then hurried over. It was then he noticed that both Dolan and Tyler had shed their coats. "Yes, Major?" he said, looking a bit puzzled.

"Lieutenant Dolan and I have a little something we need to get out of our systems. We're going out behind the barracks."

"You mean—"

"Yes. So that you can back us up when Colonel Lawson returns, you will note that we're not wearing anything that signifies rank. This dispute is between Bill Dolan and Theron Tyler, man to man. Understand?"

"Yes, sir."

"And we want privacy."

"Yes, sir."

"Thank you." Tyler gave him a tight smile and turned to enter his quarters.

Tyler and Dolan left the office by the back door and walked to the barracks. By the time they rounded the corner and headed for the rear, word had spread. Sergeant Finch had picked up enough of what Tyler had said to Thompson to know what was going on. Except for those men among the dragoons who sided with Dolan, the rest of Fort Clark would give a lot to see him knocked off his high horse.

Tyler and Dolan faced each other in the open area behind the barracks, unaware that many soldiers, and even officers' wives and children, were watching from any vantage point they could find.

For a few seconds, a deathly stillness hung in the air as the two men eyed each other.

Dolan took a step and closed the space between them. "I'm goin' to make you wish you'd stayed in Illinois, Theron ol' boy."

"You do it, then talk about it."

"You asked for it, pal."

Tyler was no novice. His first experience at fist fighting had taught him to watch his opponent's eyes. Sure enough, Dolan had signaled his rush before he moved. Tyler sidestepped quickly, causing Dolan's punch to connect with air. When Dolan planted his feet to turn, a rock-hard fist cracked his jaw. His knees gave way, and he found himself on the ground. He shook his head and cursed Tyler, rolling to his knees to get up.

Tyler waited. Dolan rushed in, both fists pumping. Tyler batted a fist aside and planted a solid punch to Dolan's nose. The stockier man took two steps back, then lunged forward, swinging a right cross.

Tyler dodged it and stumbled slightly, and before he could get his balance, Dolan chopped him a good one on the left ear. When Dolan came back with a blow to the temple, Tyler rolled with the punch, robbing it of its power. Then he stepped in with a left jab that split Dolan's upper lip and followed with a swift right uppercut. A brassy taste filled Dolan's mouth.

In a fury, Dolan caught Tyler with a powerful right that sent him staggering. Dolan charged in like a maddened bull, and put Tyler flat on his back. He kicked Tyler in the ribs and started to kick him a second time, but Tyler managed to grab Dolan's leg and topple him.

Both men jerked to their feet and traded blows for several seconds. A punch to his jaw sent Dolan down again with his head roaring like a giant waterfall. His mouth was going dry, and his breathing had become labored. But the determination to pound the major to a bloody pulp still lived within him.

He went after Tyler again, and Tyler came back with a blow to the midsection and three peppering blows to the jaw. The lieutenant reeled, trying to keep his balance. He could see three fuzzy Tylers. He chose the one in the middle and unleashed a haymaker. The major ducked it and came back with a cracking blow.

Tyler paused, fists ready. "I'd ring the bell here, Bill, but I want you to remember a few things."

Dolan kept blinking and shaking his head, hoping the gray fog would clear.

"Here's one for stealing Black Dog's body." Tyler popped him, restraining the full impact. "And this one's for murdering Spotted Coyote."

The residents of Fort Clark looked on, wondering how long before Dolan would go down for good.

Dolan's eyes were turning glassy. Tyler stung him with a series of slaps, saying they were for the five Hunkpapa warriors he had murdered. The slaps cleared the lieutenant's eyes a little, but did nothing to put strength in his watery legs.

"And this is for the sacrilege you committed against the Hunkpapas." The punch was solid and punishing, but still Dolan stood. "And this is for intimidating your own men into bending military rules."

Dolan started to buckle.

Tyler clenched his teeth, hissing the words, "And this last

one is for giving good soldiers a bad name."

The blow was so hard it lifted the lieutenant off his feet before he fell to the ground unconscious.

Tyler stood over Dolan, sucking air. "Sitting Bull…I hope this discipline was severe enough to…satisfy you."

Weeks passed. On June 25, 1853, black thunderheads gathered on the western horizon as Lieutenant Dolan and a dozen troopers—including Sergeant Leonard Cahill—rode south toward Point Nemaha. When they passed Chief Gray Shadow's Oglala village, Dolan looked with loathing across the fields at the teepees and the copper-skinned people who moved about.

The approaching storm sent gusty wind and a few pelting raindrops ahead of it. By the time the small settlement of Point Nemaha came into view, a dark curtain of rain swept across the Nebraska plains, drenching the dragoons and their horses.

Lieutenant Dolan led the column to a halt in front of the saloon. By the number of horses tied in front, he knew a good number of the settlement were inside.

Dolan dismounted and lifted his voice above the storm. "I know it's against the rules for men on a routine patrol to imbibe, but since we've got to get inside out of this storm, we'll bend the rule a bit. I know some of you won't take a drink, but I don't think you'll tattle on those of us who do."

As the soldiers dismounted, they heard the faint sound of voices from across the way. A pair of buffalo hunters seemed to be arguing with two aging Sioux Indians on the porch of the trading post.

Five of Dolan's men who chose not to drink stayed outside. Dolan wondered if the two who had ratted on him to Major Tyler were among the five abstainers.

Dolan paused, allowing a small group of farmers to file out

of the saloon, and fixed his gaze on the Indians across the way. "I don't like it that the whites in this settlement allow Indians to trade here once they're too old to be warriors."

"I suppose," Cahill said, "the whites like making money off the Indians...and when they're that old, they certainly aren't a threat to anyone."

"As far as I'm concerned, those dirty savages ought to be disposed of like rabid dogs."

Dolan moved inside and walked through a cloud of smoke. The place was noisy with loud talking and gusts of laughter. All the tables were taken, but Dolan noticed an open space at the bar and walked toward it.

A half-dozen rough-looking buffalo hunters occupied the rest of the long bar. Dolan grinned briefly and thought there was never any problem distinguishing a buffalo hunter from the rest of humanity. They all smelled of dead buffalo and campfire smoke, rancid grease, tobacco, sweat, and whiskey.

They dressed pretty much alike too—floppy broad-brimmed hats shiny with sweat, grease, and dust; ragged and faded shirts and pants that had never met soap and water; scuffed, low-heeled boots covered with blood, grease, and manure. Even in summer they wore smelly buffalo hide vests or coats, or both. They were always bearded too. Dolan guessed it was too much trouble to shave out on the plains.

While the soldiers were ordering their drinks, the buffalo hunters turned to look at them. The one next to Dolan was huge and had a smell to match his size. His eyes, narrow-set and beady, were as mean-looking as the eyes of a wild boar. Dolan decided he wouldn't want the man as an enemy.

"You fellas from Fort Clark?" The huge man grinned at Dolan, revealing yellow teeth.

Dolan nodded.

"Name's Gordo Silcox."

"I'm Bill Dolan." The lieutenant's hand wasn't small, but it felt swallowed up as he shook the other man's hand.

"Lieutenant, I see."

"Yes. And next to me is Sergeant Leonard Cahill."

Silcox nodded at Cahill, not bothering to offer his hand, then threw a thumb over his shoulder and said, "This fella next to me here is Efren Corbitt. We're both from Minnesota."

Corbitt nodded at the soldiers.

"How's the Indian situation right now, Lieutenant?" Silcox asked. He lifted his glass and downed its contents in a gulp.

"Bad."

The bartender delivered empty glasses to the soldiers and plunked down two full whiskey bottles.

"Bad?"

"Yeah. They're still alive."

The huge man guffawed. "You hate 'em that bad, eh?"

"With a passion," Dolan said, uncorking one of the bottles and pouring his glass to the brim. "Shawnees murdered my parents. I've hated Indians ever since. I'd like to exterminate every one of 'em."

"Well, I don't exactly hate 'em," Silcox said, "but I guess I would if they'd done to my parents what they did to yours."

"*I* hate 'em," Corbitt said. "I don't like always havin' to watch over my shoulder when we're skinnin' out buffalo. It's like them dirty redskins think they own everything west of the Missouri and will scalp every white man who shoots a buffalo if they can catch him unawares."

"They're sneaky, all right," Dolan said.

At Fort Clark, Major Tyler stood in the driving rain with Colonel Lawson and watched a half-dozen soldiers saddle their mounts.

"Really, Colonel," Tyler said, pulling his dark blue slicker tight at his neck, "I can make the ride to Point Nemaha by myself.

I wouldn't go at all in this rain if I hadn't promised Andrea I'd meet the army wagon train and ride back with her."

Lawson smiled, wiping rain from his face. "I appreciate a man who stands by his promise. I just don't want you out there on those plains alone. One blue coat by himself would be a tempting target for Sioux or Cheyenne warriors."

"In this rain?"

"It won't rain that long. I don't want you meeting up with a bunch of them by yourself."

"You'd make a good nursemaid, Colonel," Tyler said with a grin.

"Sometimes I wonder if that isn't what I really am—nursemaid to a bunch of infants in blue."

Tyler laughed. "Okay, okay. I shouldn't even have considered riding down there by myself."

"Now you're catching on."

It was just after ten o'clock when Tyler and his men mounted up. If Brooke's column was on schedule, they would arrive at Point Nemaha sometime late in the afternoon. Tyler meant to be there ahead of them.

"So what's the government doin' about makin' it safe in these parts?" Efren Corbitt said. "I know they're tricklin' a few more troops this way, but ain't much bein' accomplished."

"Well, you'll see more in the months to come," Dolan said. "Twenty-two new forts are under construction, and the government has plans to build that many more next year. Only the army can keep those savages in check."

"Big job," Silcox said with a grunt.

"Of course I have a better solution than just tryin' to keep those red devils in check," Dolan said.

"Oh?"

"Yeah. Be whole lot simpler just to hit all their villages and camps with heavy firepower and kill 'em all. If all the Indians were dead, we wouldn't need any forts."

When the soldiers had reached their self-imposed limit on drinks, Dolan led them outside to join the others. The rain had stopped, but the clouds still looked dark and ominous.

Farmers and their families milled about the trading post across the way. The elderly Sioux warriors and the pair of buffalo hunters were now standing in the mud near the Indians' pintos. It was obvious the Indians were trying to leave.

Lieutenant Dolan moved in that direction with his soldiers and tried to pick up the gist of the argument. Now he could clearly make out the headbands on the Indians. They were Oglalas. They had to be from Chief Gray Shadow's village.

Suddenly one of the buffalo hunters swore viciously and pulled his revolver, aiming it at the shorter Indian. The taller Indian yelled and made a move for the gun. The buffalo hunter was slow, and the old Indian got a good hold on his wrist. They grappled for a few seconds with the gun swinging wildly. Suddenly the revolver fired, and trooper Jim Pollard fell to the ground with a slug in his forehead.

Dolan swore and yanked out his sidearm, cocking back the hammer. The Indian and buffalo hunter continued to struggle with the gun while onlookers ducked.

Dolan drew up close to the combative pair, lined his gun on the Indian, and fired. The other Indian lunged for Dolan, and Dolan fired point-blank into the old man's chest.

Dolan turned to the crowd and said, "Some of you men drape the redskins over their pintos' backs." Then he turned to his soldiers, who were standing around the body of their fallen friend. "Lay Jim on his horse, men. We're takin' those two dead Indians to their village and give Gray Shadow and the rest of those stinkin' Oglalas a lesson on what happens to Indians who rise up against white men."

When the soldiers were ready to move out, Lieutenant Dolan and Sergeant Cahill bid Silcox and Corbitt goodbye.

"Ain't it dangerous for so few soldiers to go ridin' into that Sioux village with two of their dead in tow?" Silcox said. "I'd hate to hear that you and these men ended up gettin' scalped...or worse."

"We'll be fine," Dolan told him. "Those Indians fear the army. I'm just goin' to use these two vermin to teach the rest of 'em a lesson."

The wind was picking up again as Dolan and his men rode out. Sergeant Cahill rode in his usual place, next to Dolan. When they were about two miles from the Oglala settlement, he worked up his nerve to speak. "Lieutenant, sir..."

Dolan gave him a sidelong glance. "Hmm?"

"Sir, you know I'll always back you in everything you do."

"You've proven that, Lenny."

"Well, sir, maybe Silcox's concern is well founded. Maybe we ought to get some more men before we ride into that village."

"No need. Gray Shadow knows he'd pay through the nose if he laid a hand on us. There's nothin' to worry about, Lenny. Just relax."

Cahill swallowed hard and said no more.

Dolan looked off to the northeast. "Lenny, I think it would be best if we leave the road, make a circle around the village, and enter it from the east."

SIX

L aughing Horse and Curly were skinning out jackrabbits the boy had killed earlier in the morning.

"Your father is proud of you, Curly," Laughing Horse said. "You will one day be great warrior."

"That is my strongest desire, Father. I want to be as great a warrior as Fire Eagle."

"You will. Just keep practicing with your weapons and—"

Laughing Horse stopped speaking when he saw Running Deer and Little Bird slide from their horses in front of Chief Gray Shadow.

"Chief, there is a large herd of buffalo that way," Little Bird said, pointing northwest. "Many hundreds."

"How far?"

"On the banks of the Niobrara River."

A faint smile touched the chief's usually solemn mouth. "We will go."

Gray Shadow called the entire village together and told them of the great buffalo herd the scouts had sighted. He estimated the hunt would take them six or seven days.

The excitement was contagious. Nearly everyone would go. Most of the women would go to cook, and those with children would take them along. Even the old men were going, except for those few who were too feeble. The wives of the feeble ones would stay with them.

The Oglalas packed up the necessities, tying them on the horses' backs and on travois. The impending storm did not dampen the peoples' spirits. A big buffalo hunt was always a great event in their lives.

Curly started to skin the rabbits faster and to talk excitedly about the big hunt.

"You will not be going this time, my son."

"Why can I not go, Father?"

"You are needed here, since your sister is about to deliver her child, and your mother is remaining behind with her. You must stay and look after them. They will need you to help in many ways."

Disappointment clouded Curly's face. "But Father, all the other boys my age are going. They will experience great things."

At that moment, White Wing walked past and overheard her son's words. She came near him and paused. Curly met her gaze, then looked at the ground.

"Son, your father talked to me about this. I agreed that Gentle Fawn and I need you to stay with us. Your father is showing great confidence in you by leaving you here."

Curly still looked at the ground.

White Wing squeezed his shoulder. "Look at me, Son."

Slowly, Curly's dark eyes met his mother's gaze.

"Your father knows you are an expert with both musket and bow and arrow. You will be here to kill small game so the elderly who must remain behind and your sister and I will have meat. You will also be here to protect us."

Curly brightened at her words.

"Curly must show that he can obey orders," his mother continued. "Since his greatest desire is to become a great warrior, Curly must exercise discipline. Every warrior must learn to obey the orders of his superiors, or he will be a failure."

"This is true, Son," Laughing Horse said. "I am putting you to a test. I am also entrusting to your care your mother, sister, and the elderly. Is my son able to shoulder this responsibility?"

This was all Curly needed to hear. Suddenly he was proud to be chosen to stay behind. A smile spread over his face. "Yes, Father. Your son is able to shoulder the responsibility." He then cocked his head and said, "Fire Eagle did not go on the last hunt because Gentle Fawn's time to deliver draws near. Will he go this time?"

"When I was with them only moments ago," White Wing said, "Gentle Fawn was trying to persuade Fire Eagle to go. I am returning there now. I will learn how successful Gentle Fawn has been."

Laughing Horse smiled. "If our daughter is as persuasive as her mother, Fire Eagle will go."

White Wing lifted one eyebrow. "Oh? It is that simple, is it?"

"Laughing Horse has been married to White Wing for twenty-two grasses. He knows the persuasiveness of his squaw. Yes. It is that simple."

White Wing smiled and walked away.

As White Wing entered the teepee, she heard Fire Eagle's mother, Little Flower, saying, "…and my son should be at his father's side on this great hunt. Fire Eagle's mother would like to watch her son killing buffalo with the other warriors. White Wing and the elderly women who remain will be here to care for Gentle Fawn and the papoose."

"Do you see, my husband?" Gentle Fawn said, reaching for him. "I will be in the hands of Wakan Tanka and my mother, and these wise older women. Everything will be fine. Please. I want you to be by your father's side during the hunt."

Fire Eagle moved to Gentle Fawn on his knees and took her hand. He was torn between wanting to go on the hunt and wanting to be with her when she gave birth to their child. "This decision is great, sweet Gentle Fawn. It seems my place is with my father, yet at the same time, it is with you. My heart is telling me it is best that I stay with you."

Little Flower rose to her feet and laid a hand on top of her son's head. "Little Flower is very proud of her son. He has turned out to be a great warrior and sub-chief. But even more important, he is a faithful and loving husband. I know he will also be a good father to his child."

"It is my deep desire to have my husband here when our child is born," Gentle Fawn said softly, "but since I am in good hands, my deeper desire is that he take his place among the Oglala men as they provide meat and clothing for their families by hunting the buffalo."

The sub-chief lifted his wife's hand to his lips and kissed it. "Fire Eagle must think upon this alone. He will return shortly."

There was a deep ravine that ran north and south along the east side of the village for about five miles. Often Fire Eagle went there alone to meditate.

As he walked among the teepees, he smiled at the excitement of the people. Gray Shadow would be leading them out soon. He must make his decision quickly.

At the edge of the ravine, Fire Eagle stopped and stared at the grassy bottom sixty feet below. The sides of the ravine were quite steep and partially covered with brush. A hundred yards to the north and to the south, the sides of the ravine became less steep. Fire Eagle watched a small herd of antelope climbing out of the ravine where it was easier.

Finally he decided.

Gentle Fawn was on her feet, moving about, when the flap opened and Fire Eagle stepped inside.

"I will go on the hunt," he said softly. "If ever Fire Eagle needed to be *two* Fire Eagles, it is now."

"My husband has chosen correctly. He must be with the other warriors. Gentle Fawn will be fine."

Gray Shadow was happy to learn that his son would go on the hunt. Fire Eagle prepared his horse, draping buffalo hide sacks over its back that bore his bow and arrows, musket, powder, and lead balls.

As the procession was lining up to leave, Fire Eagle slipped past the flap of his teepee and found Gentle Fawn once again lying down. "Is there pain in your back?" he asked.

"Yes, but it will soon be gone. And when our child is born, Gentle Fawn will forget about the pain."

Fire Eagle looked down at her with adoring eyes. "Your beauty is like the sun dancing on the water. It is like the bow of many colors after the rain. This warrior loves you, Gentle Fawn."

"And this warrior's squaw loves him," she said.

"Wakan Tanka will watch over you until I return." Then Fire Eagle bent down and kissed her tenderly. "If the child is born while I am gone, Gentle Fawn will name him…or her."

Gentle Fawn nodded. "My love, help me up. I will come and watch you ride away."

The hunting party moved out, along with the women and children, leaving thirteen people behind—eight elderly husbands and wives, two widowed squaws, and White Wing, Gentle Fawn, and Curly.

White Wing leaned close to her daughter and said, "Do you see who is riding next to your husband?"

Gentle Fawn smiled. Red Cloud, a young Oglala who would soon be old enough to become a warrior, was at Fire Eagle's side. He had patterned himself after Fire Eagle, for he admired him above all Sioux warriors.

When the procession had passed from view, Gentle Fawn turned to her brother. "Curly, would you help Mother and me shell some corn?"

Curly took one more longing look at the procession, then smiled. "Yes, I will help you."

The corn ears were in a large wooden box near the opening of the teepee. Curly dragged it inside, then helped his sister as she eased to the ground, holding her large, uncomfortable midsection. White Wing smiled her approval of her son's care for his sister.

Outside, lightning slashed the sky. Thunder boomed in retaliation, and tiny drops of rain began to fall.

Less than an hour after Lieutenant Dolan and his patrol unit left the road to enter the forest, Major Tyler and his men trotted south toward Point Nemaha. As they came abreast of the Oglala village, Tyler commented about the lack of activity. But with all this rain, most of the Indians were probably in their teepees.

The small group of soldiers held on to their hats and bent against the wind as they watched for the familiar uneven rooftops of the Point Nemaha settlement.

Theron Tyler had missed his beautiful Andrea so much. He smiled to himself, recalling how she'd been worried he would be less attracted to her when she lost her figure. His mind drifted back to that tender moment at Fort Dillard almost eight months ago when he entered their quarters after a long day's ride...

The November air had taken on the feel of winter as he left the stables and headed for the officers' quarters. Andrea had promised him chicken and dumplings before he rode out that morning, and his mouth was starting to water at the thought. He thought his auburn-haired wife was the best cook in the world.

Before he entered their apartment he removed his hat and smoothed his thick dark hair, then opened the door. The tempting aroma of chicken and dumplings met his nostrils.

"Hello!" he called. "Is the most beautiful woman in the world back there? The most fortunate man in the world is home!"

Andrea came into the hall holding a steaming pan in her hand. She was wearing her hair in Theron's favorite style—upswept with tiny ringlets on her forehead.

"Hello, beautiful."

"Hello, fortunate," she said with a giggle.

As he started toward her, she turned and vanished through the kitchen door. Theron made a dash down the hall. When he entered the kitchen, Andrea had set the pan on the cupboard and stood waiting with a light dancing in her green eyes.

She always gave him a warm welcome home, but there was something special about her eyes and the smile on her lips.

"Okay, what is it?"

"What is *what?*"

"That look on your face. Something's up."

"Oh, I'm just so glad to have you home," she said, and flung her arms around his neck. They kissed and held each other close.

"Did you do something special with the chicken and dumplings?" he asked.

She took a step back to look into his eyes. "It's something special, all right, but it has nothing to do with the chicken and dumplings."

"Well, c'mon. Out with it."

"Maybe you'd better sit down, darling."

Theron kissed the tip of her nose. "Mrs. Tyler, I'm a battle-hardened soldier. I don't need to sit down. What is it?"

"Well…I went to Dr. Cummings today."

"Dr. Cummings? What's wrong?"

"Nothing's wrong. It's just that…well, our family is going to add another member in about seven and a half months."

Suddenly he couldn't speak. Finally, out came, "You…you're going to have a baby?"

Tears misted Andrea's eyes. "Uh-huh."

"For sure?"

"Dr. Cummings said there's no question about it."

Laughing gleefully, Theron picked up Andrea and whirled her around and around. "I'm going to be a father! I can't wait to tell the whole world!"

He planted her feet back on the floor and embraced her for a long moment. "I'm so happy!" he said. "Just think of it! You and me…parents!"

Suddenly the smile faded from Andrea's face and she laid her head on his chest.

"Hey! What's the matter?" He pushed her back to look into her eyes.

"Well…"

"Well, what?"

"I was thinking that when I get real big and lose my figure that maybe you won't find me attractive anymore. Maybe—"

"Hey, wait a minute! Listen to me."

She met his gaze and waited.

"Honey, any husband who would spurn his wife because she lost her figure carrying his baby ought to be horsewhipped. I love you, and I'm proud that you're my wife, and I'm thrilled to death that you're going to have our child. You could never be anything but beautiful to me."

Tears spilled down Andrea's cheeks as she hugged her husband tight and said, "Thank you."

"And something else, Mrs. Tyler…even if your figure never returns to what it is now, it doesn't matter to me. Though you're a beautiful woman on the outside, I love you more for what you are on the *inside*."

Thirty minutes later the rain had eased off, and only tiny raindrops were falling as the small collection of buildings that made up Point Nemaha came into view. Major Theron Tyler and his escort saw the army wagons from Fort Dillard at the same time.

"They're here already!" the major said.

With that, he put his horse to a gallop and the others were soon on his heels, dodging flying mud.

SEVEN

———•◆•———

ndrea Tyler stood on the porch of the Nemaha trading post with Lieutenant Colonel George M. Brooke and his wife, Marian.

Brooke ran his gaze to the edge of town. "I'm sure he'll be here soon, Andrea, unless he was hindered by Indian trouble or some other such thing."

Andrea shifted from one foot to another.

"Andrea, dear," Marian said, "don't you think you should sit down on that bench over there?"

"I will in a few minutes." Andrea smiled at her friend, feeling the baby move within her. "It's just that I've been sitting for so long. I need to stand for a while."

"Well, I can understand that. It sure feels good to be off that wagon seat."

The colonel's eye caught swift movement at the north end of the settlement. Seconds later he recognized Major Tyler and Sergeant Garrison and five other riders. "Andrea, here they come."

When Andrea turned and saw Theron, her eyes filled with tears. Theron saw her at the same time and raised a hand for the others to rein in as he slid off his horse.

"I've missed you something awful, sweetheart," Theron said, as he pulled her close.

"And I've missed you even more. I guess you can see, I've gotten bigger."

"Yes, and I'm glad you have. We wouldn't want our baby to be a runt!"

Andrea laughed and Theron kissed her, then kept his arm around her as he greeted Lieutenant Colonel and Mrs. Brooke and introduced his escort. The others soon went inside the trading post to give the major and Andrea a little privacy.

Tyler gestured toward a bench a few feet away. "C'mon, sweetheart. Let's sit and talk a little."

Theron fussed over Andrea to make her as comfortable as possible, then sat down and took her hand. "Tell me, really. How has the trip been?"

"Not as bad as I thought it would be. Colonel Brooke made sure I had the best of everything. I had a feather mattress in the back of my wagon, and I used it a lot, even during the day. And when I've ridden on the seat I've had pillows to make me comfortable."

"And you're feeling all right?"

"As well as can be expected. I think I must be carrying a boy. There's a lot of kicking going on in there."

Theron laughed. "If it's a girl, maybe she'll be a tomboy."

"Something like that."

After a few minutes, the men of the Fifth Infantry were gathered in front of the trading post, as were the officers, wives, and children. Major Tyler welcomed them to Nebraska Territory, then introduced those who were unacquainted.

As Tyler's escort led their horses toward the convoy, the major lifted his wife onto the seat of her wagon, and Corporal Benny Walker, a relief driver for the last leg of the trip, climbed up beside her.

Lieutenant Colonel Brooke was on horseback, as were the other four officers. The rest of the one hundred and seventeen men and the officers' wives and children rode in wagons.

The column headed north out of Point Nemaha with the lieutenant colonel and the major in the lead. Andrea Tyler's wagon followed first in line.

Corporal Walker raised his head at the sound of distant thunder. "I think we're in for more rain, ma'am."

"Sure looks like it." Andrea adjusted herself on the pillows.

"I'll do my best not to hit any bumps," he said. Then Benny set his eyes on Major Tyler. "Mrs. Tyler, that's some husband you've got."

"Don't I know it!"

"Up until he left Fort Dillard to come out here, ma'am, I spent a lot of time with the major. I've never said anything to him, but I've admired him for a long time." The young corporal's boyish sincerity touched Andrea and made her smile. "To me, ma'am, he's the epitome of a military man. It's like he was born with army blood in his veins."

"You're a lot closer to the truth than you realize," Andrea said. "As far back as his branch of Tylers can trace their family history, the Tyler men have been soldiers."

"Really?"

"Mm-hmm. My husband graduated from West Point seven years ago at the age of twenty-two. As a lieutenant, he went directly into the Mexican War. Before it was over he was promoted to captain. Two years ago, they promoted him to major."

"Not many men make major before they're thirty!"

"His father," Andrea continued, with a note of pride in her voice, "is General Thurlow Tyler. He graduated from West Point in 1826 and is now among the big brass in Washington. Theron's grandfather, Theodore Tyler, and his great-grandfather, Thaddeus Tyler, both rose to the rank of general in the British army in England."

"I guess the major comes from pretty good stock!"

"And not only is he a great military man, he's a wonderful husband."

"I could never be the soldier he is, Mrs. Tyler, since I'm not an officer, but I sure hope I have a wife someday who'll say the same thing about me as a husband."

Lightning split the sky directly overhead, immediately followed by thunder. Benny tightened the reins and talked soothingly to the horses. The wind was picking up again, and dark clouds roiled.

Benny tightened his cap on his head. "Mrs. Tyler, do you think you're going to have a boy or a girl?"

Andrea smiled. "I have a strong feeling it's a boy, but if I'm wrong and it's a girl, we'll try again. We've got to have a boy to carry on the family tradition."

"So have you and the major picked out a name?"

"Well, we've discussed several girl's names, but we haven't decided on one yet. However, if it's a boy, we've agreed the name will be *Thann.*"

"Never heard of that one. How do you spell it?"

"T-h-a-n-n. Theron made it up. You see, as far back as the family tree can be traced, every Tyler male has had a name that starts with *Th*. We could have named him after one of his forebears, but shortly after I told Theron I was with child, he came up with the name Thann. So if we have a boy, that's what we'll name him."

In the Oglala Sioux camp, four elderly warriors sat under the dark sky, talking about the white invasion of their land. Brown Fox, the youngest of the four, had once been the Oglalas' fiercest warrior. He had killed more enemies among other tribes in combat than any other Oglala warrior.

A few yards away, the warriors' squaws and two widows mended clothing.

In Fire Eagle's teepee, White Wing and Gentle Fawn were shelling corn with Curly's help.

"I overheard Father and Chief Gray Shadow talking yesterday," Curly said. "Chief Gray Shadow showed anger as he said that Sioux scouts from villages all over the territory report new forts and more soldier coats from the east."

"It seems there is not enough land in the east to satisfy the white men," White Wing said. "They want more."

Gentle Fawn looked concerned but said nothing.

Curly studied the faces of his mother and sister, animosity flashing in his eyes. "Inside Curly there lives a beast of hatred for the white eyes! Curly wishes he was old enough to be a warrior! He would kill the wicked soldier coats who steal our land and kill our buffalo!"

"No, my son! You should not carry the beast of hatred inside you! It will dry up your spirit. Our warriors fight the soldier coats to defend our land and its resources, and they kill them when they have to. But to carry hatred inside hurts the person who does the hating, not the person he hates."

"Our mother speaks great wisdom, Curly," Gentle Fawn said. "We fight the whites because they force us to, but we must not hate them."

Curly bit down hard and squeezed the ear of corn.

Tears filmed White Wing's eyes as she said, "I fear the day is coming when big battles will be fought between red men and white men. Much blood will stain our land."

Suddenly they heard Brown Fox's voice above the buffeting wind. "Soldier coats!"

Curly rushed to the opening and peered out. "Mother, many soldier coats are riding into the village!"

White Wing hurried to see for herself while Curly helped a struggling Gentle Fawn to her feet.

A column of soldiers topped the crest of the deep ravine to the east, riding two-by-two. One of them carried a white flag. When the last horses came out of the ravine, White Wing began to tremble. "There are two pintos with dead Oglalas on them!" she said. "And there is a dead soldier coat too!"

Gentle Fawn's heart started to pound. "Spotted Tail and Short Bear went into Point Nemaha to trade for goods," she said. "The soldier coats must have killed them."

"I hate soldier coats!" Curly said. "I hate them! I hate them!"

White Wing laid a calming hand on Curly's shoulder. Brown Fox and the other men stood shoulder to shoulder, watching the soldiers' approach. Brown Fox said something to the women, and they hurried toward the teepees.

"Hold it right there!" Lieutenant Dolan said.

When the women did not stop, Dolan snapped a command at two of his troopers. Sergeant Cahill and Corporal Whitman goaded their horses and dashed to block the women's path.

"You must do as Lieutenant Dolan says," Cahill said. "Go back there with the men." Reluctantly the women obeyed.

Brown Fox scowled at the lieutenant and pointed to the bodies. "Who killed Spotted Tail and Short Bear?" he asked.

"I want to talk to Gray Shadow!" Dolan said. "Get him out here right now!"

While Brown Fox explained that Gray Shadow and most of the people were away on a buffalo hunt, Gentle Fawn said in a low voice, "We must go and join them."

"No," White Wing said. "You must sit down and rest. I will go and find out what happened. Curly will stay with you."

"But the soldier coats may harm you, Mother," Curly said. "I will go find out what happened."

"You will stay with your sister." White Wing was out of the teepee before Curly could say another word.

Dolan started at the sight of another Indian, then spoke again to Brown Fox. "When will Gray Shadow and the rest of 'em be back?"

"Many days. Maybe six...seven." Brown Fox turned and walked along the column of riders until he came to the dead Oglalas. He examined the bullet holes in their chests, noting they had fallen in mud when they were shot.

Brown Fox walked back to Dolan's horse and said, "Why you kill Spotted Tail and Short Bear?"

Dolan's down-turned mouth drew into a hard line. "Those two savages murdered my trooper!"

"You lie! Those two old men would murder no one!"

Dolan spewed profanity and kicked Brown Fox in the head. The old warrior hit the ground, blood oozing from a gash on his cheek. Bull Nose rushed up and grabbed Dolan's leg, trying to pull him from the saddle. The lieutenant quickly whipped out his service revolver and cracked him over the head.

Bull Nose staggered but did not fall. He shook his head and shouted "Hokahey!" and lunged.

Dolan cracked him on the head again. This time the old man fell to his knees. Another war cry escaped his lips as he started to rise. The lieutenant snapped back the hammer, aimed at Bull Nose's chest, and pulled the trigger.

For the first time since the soldiers had ridden into camp, Curly and Gentle Fawn felt true fear.

The two remaining warriors dashed toward a pair of spears.

Dolan swore and fired his revolver, cutting down one of the Indians. "Kill 'em both, men!" he shouted.

Gunfire blended with rumbling thunder as the two warriors were peppered with bullets.

Brown Fox's squaw tried to persuade her husband not to fight back, but the warrior in him filled his heart. Gritting his teeth and setting his jaw, the old Indian ran toward the spears.

"Lieutenant, I can get off my horse and handle him if you'll give the word," Sergeant Cahill said, wanting to prevent further bloodshed.

Dolan raised his gun, dogged back the hammer, and aimed it at Brown Fox. "I'll take care of it, Sergeant."

Brown Fox lifted the spear and turned around just as Dolan squeezed the trigger. The old warrior went down. Brown Fox was still moving when his squaw ran toward him. Before she could reach him, Dolan fired another shot. Brown Fox twitched and lay still.

The squaw threw her body on top of her husband's. Dolan's eyes took on a crazy gleam as he cocked back the hammer once more and said, "So you're willin' to be a shield for him, red woman? Well, an Indian is an Indian!"

The squaw's body jerked with the bullet's impact, and she collapsed on top of her husband.

The remaining women's terrified wailing grated on Dolan's ears, so he emptied his gun into them. Still they lived. Dolan's eyes bulged as he hipped around in the saddle and screamed for his men to kill them. Most of the men were reluctant, but a few shots rang out in the falling rain and the wailing ceased.

Enraged beyond fear, White Wing found a fist-sized rock and hurled it at Dolan, hitting him on the forehead. He peeled out of the saddle and lay unconscious.

One of Dolan's men shot White Wing in the chest. From the teepee, Gentle Fawn and Curly looked on in disbelief. Was this really happening?

"I must do something, Gentle Fawn!" Curly hissed. "I must kill those horrible blue coats!"

"No! There is nothing you can do, Curly! They will kill you, too! We must escape while we can."

"Escape where?"

"The ravine! We will hide there!"

Brother and sister held hands, and Curly did what he could to help her. They had barely left the camp when they heard one of the soldiers command a search.

"Hurry!" Gentle Fawn gasped. "If they find us, they will kill us!"

Rain stung their faces as they struggled toward the ravine. A bolt of lightning crackled through the low-hanging clouds, turning the whole area bright white for a few seconds. When the lightning was gone, the ravine looked up at them like a bottomless black maw, but it offered their only measure of safety.

CHAPTER

EIGHT

———◆———

I'll go in front of you. If you slip, I can break your fall!" Curly said.

Gentle Fawn supported her heavy midsection with one hand and tried to wipe the rain from her eyes. She glanced toward the village and saw the soldiers dashing from teepee to teepee.

Curly stepped in front of his sister. "Put your arms around my shoulders. I will hold onto the bushes to keep us from going down too fast."

Lightning rent the sky, giving a brief display of the wet, grassy bottom sixty feet below. Gentle Fawn held onto her brother and followed him down the steep slope. Twice Curly's feet went out from under him, but each time he managed to keep them from falling.

When they were almost halfway, there was no more brush to hold onto. Curly turned to help Gentle Fawn sit down. The instant he let go of the bush, his feet slipped as if he were on ice. Both Curly and Gentle Fawn went down hard. Curly grabbed for her, but Gentle Fawn tumbled to the bottom. When Curly reached her, Gentle Fawn was holding her midsection and sucking air through her teeth.

"Is it bad?" Curly asked, worry etching his features.

She nodded and gasped.

"Gentle Fawn, I will try not to hurt you, but I must get you over there next to those bushes so the soldier coats cannot see you if they should look down here."

She nodded again. Thunder shook the earth as Curly took hold of Gentle Fawn's arms and dragged her across the wet grass. When they reached the nearest clump of bushes, he helped her crawl in as far as possible. Above the roar of the pounding rain and his sister's moans, Curly could hear the lieutenant command his men to mount up and head back to the fort.

Curly leaned close to Gentle Fawn, who was gritting her teeth in pain. "Sister, the soldiers are leaving!"

"Go…go up there and see about Mother. She or…some of the others…might still be alive."

"But I mustn't leave you."

"I will be all right. Please…if somehow Wakan Tanka has kept our mother alive—"

A spasm of pain rocked her.

"Gentle Fawn! I cannot leave you!"

"You must! Please! Go see about them."

"All right, I will go. And I will hurry back to you."

Curly got a good run at the rain-drenched slope. He slipped several times, but finally reached the crest and dashed toward the village.

The sharp, stabbing pains in Gentle Fawn's abdomen told her the baby was ready to come. Icy fear clawed at her. She needed help to give birth, and she knew she could never climb out of the ravine.

"Oh, Wakan Tanka! Please! Please do not let my child die!"

The pintos still stood where the soldiers had left them with Spotted Tail and Short Bear draped over their backs, the rain sluicing off their bodies. The other Indians lay where they had fallen. Curly spied his mother and ran to her. She was still breathing, but she lay very still.

"Mother! Mother, can you hear me?" Curly wept at the sight of the blood on her buckskin dress. He knew nothing about removing a bullet. If he tried and did it wrong, he could kill her.

He darted from body to body, trying to see if anyone else was still alive. All were dead except for Bull Nose. The old warrior was unconscious and bleeding profusely from his chest wound.

A surge of hatred boiled up in Curly. He could feel himself killing the lieutenant with his bare hands. "Lieutenant Dolan," they had called him. He would never forget.

Curly hurried back to his mother. His heart quickened when he saw her roll her head and blink.

"Mother! Can you hear me?"

White Wing blinked again and attempted to focus on her son. "Curly. Gentle Fawn. Is...is she all right?"

"She is fine, Mother."

"Where is she?"

"She...she's at the bottom of the ravine. We went there to hide from the soldier coats. They are gone now."

Curly shielded his mother's eyes from the rain as she spoke faintly. "Is...is anyone else...alive?"

"Only Bull Nose." Curly looked at the old warrior. "At least he was a moment ago. He is not conscious."

"Curly...you must go and help Gentle Fawn. She must be inside...teepee, out of rain."

"I will first get you and Bull Nose inside. Does the wound hurt bad, Mother?"

"It burns like fire, Son."

Curly eyed the circle of crimson. It did not seem to be spreading. "I think it is not bleeding right now, Mother. It may hurt some for me to move you, but I must get you out of the rain and wind."

Curly dragged White Wing to the teepee. The strain on her

body brought on more pain, and it looked as though the wound might be bleeding again. But the dress was so wet, Curly couldn't tell.

He went back to drag Bull Nose inside and then knelt beside his mother. White Wing's eyes were closed, but the touch of her son's hand brought them open.

"Bull Nose is still alive, Mother. He is not yet conscious. I have laid him right over here, close to you."

White Wing nodded. "Go, now, Son. Help your sister. Bring her...here. I want...to see her."

"I will be back very soon with Gentle Fawn, Mother," Curly said. "Do you need anything before I go?"

"Water," she said, running her tongue over dry lips.

Curly hurried to a wooden bucket and filled the long-handled dipper. He gave his mother as much water as she wanted, then ran from the teepee.

Gentle Fawn's pains had grown worse during Curly's absence. She tried not to let on as her brother slid down the slope toward her.

"Mother is still alive, Gentle Fawn! She has a bullet in her chest, but she was able to talk to me. Bull Nose is the only other one alive. I put both of them in the teepee."

"You must go and help her, Curly. Cut the dress away from the wound and press a clean cloth to it. Change the cloth often if she is bleeding much. Do the same for Bull Nose. It is up to you to treat them, Curly. You must not let them bleed to death."

"Mother wants me to bring you to the teepee, Gentle Fawn."

A labor pain shot through her. She jerked and let out a small cry.

"You are hurting, Gentle Fawn! I must get you into the teepee!"

Gentle Fawn shook her head and spoke through clenched teeth. "Curly...I cannot make the...climb. Ungh-h-h!"

"Gentle Fawn! Are you going to have the baby now?"

Gentle Fawn feared her brother would not leave her to tend their mother if he knew the truth. "The baby is coming soon," she said, "but it is not possible to say when. I have much pain from the fall. You must go back to Mother and Bull Nose."

"I wish to kill the lieutenant and the rest of the dirty soldier coats. I wish Wakan Tanka would let me kill them!"

"You must not think of the lieutenant and his soldier coats, Curly. Go! Take care of Mother and Bull Nose."

Curly slowly rose to his feet. "But those soldier-coat snakes must pay for what they did! I hate them more than I hate all our other enemies!"

Another painful spasm struck Gentle Fawn. Her voice was low and guttural as she commanded him, "You must go! Now!"

Curly wheeled and ran toward the steep slope. Gentle Fawn watched him slip and slide and fight his way to the top. When he reached it, he turned once and looked back, then disappeared.

Gentle Fawn felt her head go light, and everything seemed to whirl in circles. Her breath was coming fast and irregular now. Another spasm hit, and she started to cry out, but this time the cry locked in her throat.

She had known for months the delivery would be a dangerous one, but White Wing would be there when the baby came and had assured Gentle Fawn that she and the baby would be fine. Now she was sure they would die.

Gentle Fawn closed her eyes and willed a veil of calm to settle over her. She was glad Fire Eagle had gone on the hunting trip. If he had been in the village today, he would now be dead.

She steeled herself against the gray fog descending over her brain. "Please, Sky Father. Do not let me pass out or we will both die! Oh, Wakan Tanka, help me!"

Her cry for help reminded her of the day that Paul Breland,

who had lived among them, read from the white man's book—the Bible. The elderly missionary had taught them to speak English by reading the Bible. He had insisted it was not only the white man's book, but had been given to all men by the Sky Father, whom Breland called God.

That day he had assisted in the birth of an Oglala baby, and he wanted them to know why bringing a child into the world caused so much physical pain. He told them that the first man and woman—Adam and Eve—had sinned against God. He showed them these words from the holy Book:

Unto the woman he said, I will greatly multiply thy sorrow and thy conception; in sorrow thou shalt bring forth children.

Paul Breland had then explained how this affliction fell not only on Eve, but on all mothers who came after her. He told the Oglalas of God's Son born on the other side of the earth many centuries ago. The birth of Jesus Christ was like no other, for His mother had conceived and given birth as a virgin, the Father being the Sky Father—God—Himself.

Jesus Christ had died and shed His blood on a wooden cross to provide the only way for sinful human beings of all races to be forgiven their transgressions against God and to go to His Sky House when they died.

He told the Oglalas with tears in his eyes that they must believe God's Word and put their faith in Jesus Christ or they would be locked up forever in the awful place of eternal fire.

The Oglala medicine men had argued, saying it was good that Breland was teaching them English, but they had their own beliefs about death and eternity. They did not need white man's Book nor white man's God and His Son.

Gentle Fawn was fourteen grasses at the time, and even though the adults in the tribe assured her the white man was wrong, she had not been able to shrug off his words.

Breland had died soon after, right in the Oglala village. Just before he took his last breath he told Gentle Fawn that he wanted her to have his Bible. She still kept it in a wooden box in her teepee. She had read it from time to time, but it made her confused about her own religion. Finally she put the Bible away to read it no more

Gentle Fawn thought of the amazing peace Paul Breland had shown in his hour of death, and then she summoned every ounce of mental strength she could to force thoughts of the white man's Jesus from her mind. She must be faithful to her Lakota religion. Her life and the life of the baby within her were in the hands of the Sky Father, who had no son, and Ynke-lo, the god of death.

As pain ripped through her body, she tried to stifle her cry, realizing for the first time that if Curly heard it, he would leave their mother and come to her. This must not happen.

But the cry wrenched its way from her in a loud scream and was carried away by the wind. Would she live to have Fire Eagle hold her in his arms again? Would his child live to know him?

NINE

———◆———

Curly had seen dead people before. As he knelt beside Bull Nose and placed an open palm close to his mouth, he could feel no breath; neither was there a rise and fall of Bull Nose's chest.

Curly crawled back to his mother and found her licking her lips and moving her head back and forth. The stain around the bullet hole was growing larger.

"Mother...Bull Nose is dead."

White Wing rolled her head toward the old warrior. Her brow furrowed.

"Mother, you are bleeding again. Gentle Fawn told me to use a clean cloth to—"

"Where is she?" White Wing's eyes searched the teepee.

"She is in the ravine, Mother. It is...too wet for her to climb out. I am afraid to try it. She could...she could fall and hurt herself. But I will do what she told me. I must stop your bleeding."

"Is she all right?"

"She is fine, Mother. She is lying beneath a heavy bush, trying to stay out of the wind."

"But...she is soaking wet. We have to help her."

"It is not good that she is wet, Mother, but right now the

most important thing is to get this bleeding stopped. I must do this."

White Wing was too weak to argue.

Curly gave her another drink of water, then went to work on the wound. The hatred in him, especially toward the lieutenant called Dolan, grew deeper.

The baby was coming! In the midst of her agony, Gentle Fawn knew instinctively that the pressure below her waist was the child struggling to push its way into the world.

A powerful pain spread through her midsection and splintered down her legs and all the way to the top of her head. She saw a shower of bright-colored stars, then felt herself begin to go numb.

Gentle Fawn fought with every ounce of strength to keep from passing out. She gritted her teeth and emitted a nasal whine that became a shrill scream. When she opened her eyes and blinked through the haze, a tall wraithlike shape appeared before her. Was it Ynke-lo coming to take her?

The lightning flashes gave Gentle Fawn a few seconds to focus on the dark figure. It was not Ynke-lo. It was a man in a shiny black slicker that flapped in the wind.

The man knelt beside her. Momentary light showed Gentle Fawn the face of a dark-haired white man. He wore a black, flat-crowned hat and was looking at her with compassionate gray eyes.

When he laid a hand on her shoulder and spoke in a soft, resonant voice above the sound of the storm, she knew he was real.

"I was riding the ridge of the ravine," he said in her Lakota language. "I heard you scream. You are about to give birth, I see."

Gentle Fawn swallowed with difficulty and nodded.

His appearance had cleared her mind to a degree, and her

words tumbled out now. "I...expected difficult birth...was not supposed to be in ravine. No one to help."

The man spoke in a calm voice as rain dripped off his hat brim. "Ma'am, I'm not a medical doctor, but I've delivered babies on several occasions. I believe I'm the only help you have. If you'll give me permission, I'll take over and we'll get this baby born."

Gentle Fawn remembered reading in the Bible about angels from the white man's heaven who helped poor earthly mortals. She recalled that the Bible depicted them as looking exactly like men.

Gentle Fawn nodded and said in English, "Please...help me. Thank you."

The tall man examined the baby's position and said, "You'll have to do your part, little mother. Don't pass out on me now. I need your help to push the baby out."

Fiery daggers of lightning and cannonades of thunder ran a strange counterpoint to the young woman's pain and the white man's encouraging words.

Gentle Fawn's body hurt like nothing she had ever felt in her life. The gray cloud that threatened to take over was closing in rapidly, and she had no more strength to fight it. The man's voice sounded far away as he repeatedly told her to push.

One bolt of lightning followed another now, and a series of thunderous roars rolled across her ears. Gentle Fawn kept a slight hold on consciousness, but like the man's voice, the rumbling seemed to fade into the distance. Soon the pounding rain was gone from her hearing, and all she could distinguish was the thunder, like the firing of faraway cannons. *Quiet thunder...quiet thunder...quiet thunder.* The words repeated over and over in her brain.

As she felt one final searing pain, a black curtain started to descend but abruptly lifted when she felt tremendous relief in her lower body. She heard the distinct smack of palm against skin, followed by the shrill cry of her newborn baby. "It's a healthy, husky boy, ma'am!" the man said.

Gentle Fawn thought of Fire Eagle. He would be so happy!

The stranger tied the umbilical cord and cut it, then used rainwater from a shallow puddle to wash the baby.

The sky was clearing as Gentle Fawn held her newborn son in her arms, wrapped in a blanket the white man had taken out of his bedroll. She sat on the ground under the man's slicker.

"Now, tell me," he said, "why you are down in this ravine and not up there inside a nice dry teepee."

Gentle Fawn briefly explained about the buffalo hunt. She described the horrible slaughter of the elderly Indians who had remained behind, and how her mother—who had stayed to help her deliver the baby—was shot down and left for dead. Her brother, Curly, was in camp with her mother right now.

"As soon as you feel up to it," the man said, "you can ride my horse out of the ravine. I noticed that it's not so steep back there a ways."

"In a few moments," she said.

The man nodded. "I do not know your name."

"I am Gentle Fawn, squaw of Sub-Chief Fire Eagle, son of Chief Gray Shadow. I am daughter of Laughing Horse and White Wing. May I ask how you know the Lakota tongue?"

"It's a long story, ma'am," he said with a grin. "There isn't time to tell it right now."

"Then, may I ask…are you an angel sent down from white man's heaven?"

The tall man grinned again. "You know about angels, do you?"

"Yes. We had a missionary here some years ago. He taught us English and read to us from his Bible. He died in our village and gave his Bible to me."

"Did he read to you about the Lord Jesus Christ and about His death on the cross…and His resurrection…and the salvation He gives from sin and the wrath of God?"

"Yes, but we Lakota have our own religion."

"So none of you accepted what the missionary told you about Jesus?"

"No. My father is a medicine man."

"Do you ever read the Bible the missionary left you?"

"I did for a while, but it made me doubt my Lakota religion, so I stopped." She paused, then said, "You did not answer my question, sir. Are you one of those angels spoken of in the Bible?"

"No, Gentle Fawn, I am not an angel."

"But the Sky Father sent you at just the right time to deliver my baby. That I am sure of. Both of us would have died without you. Are you a missionary then?"

"Not in the sense you are thinking. I do travel about and preach the Word of God, but my work is broader than that."

"What is your name?"

There was a gleam in the tall man's eye as he replied, "Folks call me John Stranger."

The baby began to fuss. "I think your little boy is hungry, ma'am," Stranger said. "Why don't you feed him while I go and get my horse? Then, if you're up to it, we'll get you back to camp so you can see about your mother."

Early afternoon sun was breaking through the clouds as Curly dragged the lifeless form of Bull Nose from the teepee and placed it beside the other bodies.

His heart was heavy for his mother. She had been unconscious for some time. He had successfully slowed the bleeding, but he knew that if the bullet was not removed soon, she would die of lead poisoning.

Curly glanced toward the ravine. He would go and check on Gentle Fawn. Perhaps if he could help her out of the ravine, she could remove the bullet. But first he would see if his mother was awake.

When he found White Wing still unconscious, he dashed outside and ran east, weaving his way through the teepees. Movement caught his eye and he skidded to a stop as he saw his sister sitting on a blaze-faced bay gelding, holding a small bundle. A tall white man dressed in black led the horse, and they were headed straight for him. Gentle Fawn showed no sign of fear.

Curly ran to them and looked at the angular face of the stranger, then back to Gentle Fawn.

The man kept moving as Curly walked alongside and smiled up at his sister. "Is the baby all right?"

"Yes, my brother. You have a healthy nephew."

"A boy! Good! As son of the mighty Fire Eagle, he will one day be a great warrior! Is Gentle Fawn all right?"

"Yes, but the baby and I would be dead if it were not for this man. His name is John Stranger. Wakan Tanka sent him along the edge of the ravine at just the right time. He heard me scream and came to my rescue. He knew exactly what to do to deliver the baby."

"I thank you, Mr. John…Stranger," Curly said. "Are you a medicine man—I mean, a doctor?"

"No, but I have delivered a good number of babies in my time."

"How does our mother fare, Curly?"

"She still lives, but Bull Nose is dead. Mother has been unconscious since not long after I left you. I was able to slow the bleeding, but the bullet must be removed soon."

"I know about bullet wounds," Stranger said. "Do you mind if I look at her?"

Stranger followed Curly to Gentle Fawn's teepee, noting the line of corpses nearby. Gentle Fawn eyed them and looked away.

Stranger moved up beside the horse and raised his arms. "You hold onto the papoose, Gentle Fawn. I'll lift you down the same way I put you in the saddle."

The young mother clutched the tiny bundle to her breast as Stranger lifted her and set her on the ground. She took two steps and almost went down, but Stranger caught her.

Inside the teepee, Gentle Fawn was glad to see the rise and fall of White Wing's chest, but she was still unconscious.

Curly brought a pallet from the other side of the teepee and laid it a few feet from his mother. "There, my sister," he said. "You lie down here."

As Stranger helped Gentle Fawn onto the pallet, she said, "Curly, over there in that canvas bag are some blankets I made just for the baby. Will you bring me one? You will find body cloths, also. Bring me one of those too, please."

Stranger knelt beside White Wing and marveled at how much Gentle Fawn resembled her. He removed Curly's blood-soaked cloth and examined the wound closely.

"What do you think, John Stranger?" Gentle Fawn asked as she removed the large blanket from the baby and proceeded to wrap him in one she had made.

"From what I see, she has lost a lot of blood. But her chances are good if I can get the slug out, though there's a certain amount of risk involved. The two of you will have to tell me whether or not to go ahead."

"She will die if you do not remove the bullet?" Gentle Fawn asked.

Stranger nodded.

"Then you must go ahead, John Stranger," Gentle Fawn said. "If you are as good at bullet removals as you are at difficult baby deliveries, Mother will be fine."

"All right. I have a medical kit in my saddlebags. I'll be right back."

While Stranger was at his horse, Curly reached down and

pulled away the blanket to look at the sleeping baby. "Such a handsome boy, my sister. Fire Eagle will be proud. Have you chosen a name yet?"

"No. I must think on it awhile."

"He has much thick black hair. Maybe you should call him Black Wolf."

Gentle Fawn let a smile tug at the corners of her lips. "That is a good name, but I must think on it longer."

"Black Cloud? We have Red Cloud."

"Another good name, but it does not fit. I will know the right name when it comes to mind."

Stranger returned, carrying a small black bag and a tin flask marked "Wood Alcohol." He cleaned his hands with it, then produced a scalpel and a large pair of tweezers. He paused and looked at the brother and sister. "Before I begin, I'm going to call on my God to help me," he said.

CHAPTER

The way John Stranger prayed reminded Gentle Fawn of Paul Breland. There was no chanting or loud, high-pitched wailing, as when the Lakota medicine men prayed.

White man's God has better ears than Lakota god, Gentle Fawn thought, then instantly felt guilty.

Stranger cut away White Wing's buckskin blouse on each side of the bullet hole and cleaned the area with alcohol, then cleaned the scalpel and tweezers. Gentle Fawn and Curly watched his steady hands dig into the blood-filled hole. After a few minutes, Curly turned his head.

"What is wrong?" his sister whispered.

"I have seen blood before, but when it is the blood of someone I love, it is too much for me."

Gentle Fawn smiled and mussed his curly hair. "Even though my little brother will one day be a warrior, it is good to know he has a soft place deep inside."

"She is my mother."

"And if it were your sister lying there, would you be able to watch?"

Curly's face flushed. "No. Curly loves his sister as much as he loves his mother, only in a different way."

Gentle Fawn reached out and stroked Curly's cheek. "And Gentle Fawn loves her brother very, very much."

Soon John Stranger pulled out the slug and dropped it on the dirt floor, then took up needle and thread. When the wound was sutured, he cleaned the area again with alcohol, then bandaged it.

"You should have been a doctor, John Stranger."

He looked at Gentle Fawn and smiled. "God had other plans for me."

"How do you know this? Does your Sky Father God come and talk with you?"

"Not so that I hear Him with my ears," John said, turning back to his work. "He has a way of speaking to a Christian with, shall I say, a still, small voice in our hearts. He also speaks to a Christian through His Book, the Bible. Let me tell you something else about my God, Gentle Fawn."

"Yes?"

"He became a Man."

"I read that in the missionary's Bible," she said. "It is Jesus Christ, whom it says was born of a virgin."

"That's right. Isaiah 7:14 says His name is Emmanuel— "God with us." He was God walking among men, and He is still God right now as He sits in heaven. He is up there, looking down at this human race, Gentle Fawn. He is extending His loving hands to a lost world, asking them to come to Him."

The conversation had turned in a direction that made Gentle Fawn think, once again, that Jesus Christ might really be who the Bible said He was. But she wondered how he could be the Sky Father and yet be the Sky Father's Son. She wasn't about to ask. Rather, she rose to her knees with the baby cradled in one arm and examined White Wing's bandage. "That is good, John Stranger."

The tall man rose to his feet, went to the water pail, and poured some water in a metal pan beside it. As he began washing his instruments, he said, "Your mother seems to be a strong person. I can't guarantee that she will live, but I think she will. It will depend on how much blood she's lost."

"She will live," Gentle Fawn said. "I know it because the Sky Father sent you here to us. Just as the Sky Father used you to save my life and that of my little son, you were sent here to save the life of our mother. You said you are not an angel, but I think you are. Do you not think so, Curly?"

Curly nodded.

"The Lord Jesus also sent me here to tell you about Him," Stranger said. "I'm headed on a special mission to some people in the mountains of Wyoming Territory. These people desperately need my help. But before I go I'd like to read to you from my Bible and—"

Suddenly the baby began to fuss. Gentle Fawn looked up at Stranger and her brother. "I must ask you two to leave the teepee while I feed my son."

While Gentle Fawn nursed her newborn, she stroked his little face. "Your father is going to be so proud of you. You will grow up to be a great warrior, just like him."

She glanced at her mother, who lay still, breathing evenly, then turned back to her boy. "It is time for me to give you your name." She bent and kissed the baby's forehead. "My little son, your name is Quiet Thunder."

Although the Army wagon train moved slowly, Andrea Tyler was experiencing pain. She didn't want to alarm her husband unduly and decided not to say anything until she was sure it was labor pain. A little more time would tell.

Corporal Benny Walker noticed her grimace and arch her back. "Are you hurting, Mrs. Tyler?"

"A little," she said, trying to smile.

"Do you think the baby's coming?"

"I'm not sure."

"Do you want me to call the major?"

"No. It could be false labor. Maybe I should lie down for a while."

"Okay. I'll stop the wagon."

"No need for that," Andrea said, rising from the seat. "I can do it with the wagon moving."

"Yes, ma'am." Benny steadied her as she crawled through the opening.

Lieutenant Colonel Brooke and Major Tyler rode side by side some thirty yards ahead of Andrea's wagon. Tyler was scanning the broad prairie with binoculars.

"What about the Indians in this area, Major Tyler? Are they all hostile?"

"Well, sir, most of the time we don't have any serious trouble. But on occasion they do go on the warpath. It happens over the killing of their buffalo more than anything else."

"From what I've been told," Brooke said, "there are multiplied thousands of buffalo out here. I would think the comparative few the whites kill wouldn't make any difference."

"It's not only that the whites kill the buffalo, sir, it's the waste. The Indians use every part of the buffalo for something. When they see whites just skin them out and take the hide, leaving the carcasses to rot, they get angry. And of course they look at us as intruders and trespassers. So when we kill their buffalo, they take offense."

"Well, I guess we can't blame them."

"That's the way I look at it, sir. After all, they were here first. Wouldn't we fight back if we were in their place?"

"Most assuredly."

"I'm glad you see it that way. Some men in this army hate the Indians just because they fight back and use tactics that seem harsh and cruel to us. But they're simply fighting back the only way they know how."

Tyler twisted around to check on Andrea. "Excuse me, sir, I need to go back and see if my wife is all right. She's gone into the back of the wagon."

Tyler trotted back to Corporal Walker. "Is Mrs. Tyler all right, Corporal?"

"She was having some discomfort, sir, so she decided to lie down for awhile."

"But she's okay?"

"Yes, sir. I'm sure she would have said if there was anything wrong."

"All right. I know she's worn out from this long trip. She'll get some rest when we get to the fort."

As Tyler rode back to Lieutenant Colonel Brooke, the clouds were separating, letting the sun shine through.

John Stranger and Curly stood over the bodies of the slain Oglalas. Stranger knew the Sioux custom of placing the dead on pole scaffolds and he'd spotted them at the edge of the village.

"You will want these bodies on the scaffolds, won't you, Curly?"

"Yes. I must place them there before the sun goes down. I have been wondering how to do this by myself."

"You won't have to," John said. "I'll help you."

Curly smiled. "You are not like most white men, John Stranger."

When the job was done, Curly said, "John Stranger, it would be good if you could stay with us until Chief Gray Shadow and my father return."

"I wish I could, Curly, but my mission is pressing. I must get to those people in the mountains as soon as possible. I will leave medicine for White Wing and instruct you and your sister how to care for her."

When Stranger and the boy approached the teepee, Curly called out, "My sister…"

"Yes, come in."

The baby lay asleep in the cradle Fire Eagle had made. Gentle Fawn was kneeling over her mother, who was conscious, giving her a drink of water.

Curly let out a happy cry. "Oh, Mother, you are going to be all right!"

White Wing turned languid eyes on her son and offered him a faint smile. She then lifted her gaze to the tall man. She tried to speak, but could barely whisper.

Gentle Fawn touched White Wing's lips. "I told Mother, John Stranger, that you saved her life by removing the bullet. I also told her how you saved my life and the baby's. She wants to thank you."

"No need to thank me, ma'am. I just did what any man would have done."

"Not any *white* man," Gentle Fawn said.

"Mother," Curly said, "he helped me put the bodies of the old people on the scaffolds. I wish he could stay for a long, long time, but he says he has to leave."

"Can you not stay the night, John Stranger?" Gentle Fawn asked. "I will prepare you a good meal. You can sleep in one of the teepees. I will feed you again in the morning, then you can go your way."

"I wish I could take you up on the generous offer, Gentle Fawn, but I really must go. I will leave you medicine and more bandages for your mother."

Gentle Fawn nodded and rose to her feet. It took the tall man only a few minutes to teach her how to care for her mother's wound. Then he said, "Before I go, may I read to you from the Bible?"

Gentle Fawn did not really want to hear from the Book that made her doubt her tribe's religion, but she would not offend this man.

"How about if I read from *your* Bible, Gentle Fawn? The one the missionary left you."

She turned to her brother. "Curly, would you bring me the Bible from the wooden box over there?"

Curly rummaged around for a few moments and produced the Bible. Some of the pages were bent. Gentle Fawn took it from Curly, worked at straightening the cover and pages, then handed it to Stranger.

The three Indians listened intently as Stranger read several passages on salvation, pointing out each time that there was only one way to be saved, and that was through the Lord Jesus Christ. He would then ask if they understood.

Stranger could tell by their answers that Gentle Fawn was the only one who came near grasping it, but it would take more than this one time to get the gospel message through to her. With White Wing and Curly, it would take even longer. Stranger wished he had more time to spend with them, but he could tarry no longer. He closed the Bible and said, "Gentle Fawn, will you make me a promise?"

"What is that?"

"Will you read this Book and ask God to open your heart to His truth?"

"I must be honest with you, John Stranger. When the missionary read it to me, it made me afraid—even as it has just now."

"Because it speaks different than what you have been taught in the Lakota religion. Is that it?"

"Yes."

Curly and White Wing looked on in silence.

"I understand, Gentle Fawn," Stranger said, "but if you will read this book, asking God to open your heart, you will find the truth."

"I will read it, John Stranger," Gentle Fawn said.

———◆———

The army wagon train was near the halfway mark between Fort Clark and Nemaha when Lieutenant Colonel Brooke noticed Major Tyler studying the land to his right through binoculars. Brooke squinted but saw only rolling prairie and a dense forest.

"What is it, Tyler?"

"Gray Shadow's Oglala village is over there, sir. You'll see it in another minute or two. It's just north of the forest's edge, along a deep ravine."

"Oh, yes. I see it now. Lots of teepees, that's for sure."

Tyler peered through the binoculars again. "Something's happened over there, sir."

"What do you mean?"

"There's hardly anyone in the village. Most of the horses are gone, too."

"Is that unusual?"

"Maybe not, sir, but I can make out two men...wait a minute, a man and a boy. A *white* man and an Indian boy. They're lifting a body onto a death scaffold, and I can see several other bodies on scaffolds. It isn't normally allowed for a white man to observe such a thing, much less take part in it. Sir, I'd like to ride into the village and see what's happened."

"You mean alone?"

"Yes, sir. You can keep moving. I'll catch up."

Brooke shook his head. "Can't let you do it, Major."

"But, sir, if they need help, this would be a good opportunity to improve our relations with them—show them we're not as bad as they might think."

"Major, I'll only approve of such a move if we swing the whole wagon train in there. That way, if there are some warriors you haven't seen, and they take offense at our intrusion, they'll see all these soldiers and stay peaceful."

"Fine, sir. I'll ride back and explain it to the others."

"Before you go, John Stranger, would you like to know what I named Fire Eagle's son?" Gentle Fawn asked.

"You have named him?" Curly blurted.

Gentle Fawn explained how the booming thunder during the baby's birth seemed to fade into the distance until it was only a quiet sound. "So," she said, smiling, "I have named him Quiet Thunder."

White Wing spoke in a faint whisper, "That is a beautiful name, my daughter. Fire Eagle will like it."

"Curly likes it, too," the boy said.

"And I like it," Stranger said. "Quiet Thunder has a good sound."

Tears misted Gentle Fawn's eyes. "Fire Eagle would never have known his son if it were not for you, John Stranger. You have truly been sent to us by the Sky Father."

"Then you will read His Book for me, won't you?"

Gentle Fawn was about to tell him once more that she would, when the sounds of rattling harness and blowing horses met her ears.

Curly dashed to the opening. "It is soldier coats! Many of them!"

Stranger peered out a moment later and relaxed.

"I will get my gun!" Curly said. "They are not going to kill the rest of us! You will help me, won't you, John Stranger?"

"No need for your gun, Curly," Stranger said. "There are women and children in those wagons. The soldiers wouldn't ride in here intending to use their weapons with the women and children along."

The sound of the wagons grew louder as the army train rolled into the village. Gentle Fawn could see two mounted soldiers looking around. She moved to the cradle and laid Quiet Thunder in it. "We must go out and talk to them, Curly."

Stranger was helping White Wing sit up and sip some water, but even that small amount made her cough. He began to pat her back gently while saying to Gentle Fawn, "You are too weak to stand on your feet. Lie down next to your mother and let Curly tell the soldiers you are in the teepee. Let the soldiers come to you. They will not harm Curly."

"I cannot lie down, John Stranger. I am daughter-in-law of Chief Gray Shadow and wife of Sub-Chief Fire Eagle. It is my duty to meet them and ask what they want."

"All right, Gentle Fawn," Stranger said. "You go on out. I'll stay with your mother."

ELEVEN

———◆———

A ndrea Tyler rose to her knees to watch her husband and Lieutenant Colonel Brooke veer off the road across undulating prairie. Corporal Walker followed suit and the wagon lurched as it left the road.

Andrea let out a moan.

"I'm sorry, Mrs. Tyler. That hump was there and I couldn't avoid it. Are you all right?"

"I will be in a moment."

"Are you sure, ma'am? If you're hurting bad, I'll stop the wagon and call the major."

"No. I'll be fine, Benny. Thank you."

Maybe we'll make it to the fort before the baby comes, and maybe we won't, Andrea thought. Especially since they were taking a detour to the Indian village. She hadn't understood all of Theron's words to Benny Walker, but she caught that there were several dead Indians and almost no one moving around.

She tried to get more comfortable on the mattress while staying on her knees so she could watch their approach. She had a passing thought that the Oglalas had set a trap for the army wagon train. She quickly dismissed the thought, knowing that her husband would have warned Brooke if there was the remotest chance of that.

Andrea felt a sharp pain lance through her abdomen just as Theron came riding alongside the wagon.

"You all right, darlin'?" he asked.

"A bit uncomfortable," she said. "But I'm fine. I heard you say something to Benny about dead Indians."

"Yes. Do you know what a death scaffold is?"

"No."

Theron explained the Sioux custom.

"So through your binoculars you saw some bodies on these scaffolds?"

"Several of them. And I saw a white man and an Indian boy placing them. That just isn't the way the Indians do it. Something's wrong. This may be an opportunity to show the Oglalas that we want to help them if we can."

The lowering sun glittered in a cobalt blue sky as Gentle Fawn and Curly walked toward the men on horseback. Andrea asked Benny Walker to help her climb onto the wagon seat. She had noticed that the Indian boy was almost holding the woman up.

"You talk to them, Major," Brooke said.

"I hope there's somebody here who speaks English," Tyler replied. "Otherwise it's going to be sign language."

Tyler dismounted and touched his hat brim and smiled as he spoke to Gentle Fawn. "Ma'am, do you speak English?"

"Yes," she responded warily.

Tyler did not like the boy's ferocious expression. "Ma'am, I am Major Theron Tyler of Fort Clark. This is Lieutenant Colonel George Brooke. He has led this wagon train from the east country, and we are headed for the fort right now. I noticed as we were passing that a white man and a boy were placing bodies on scaffolds."

"Yes."

"We noticed, ma'am, that there was no one else moving about, and that most of the horses are gone. I decided something was wrong. We have come into the village to offer help, if you need it."

"Major Tyler, I am Gentle Fawn, squaw of Sub-Chief Fire Eagle, and this is my brother, Curly."

"Then you are daughter-in-law of Chief Gray Shadow," Tyler said. "I know that Fire Eagle is his son."

Gentle Fawn nodded. "Chief Gray Shadow has led most of our people on a buffalo hunt. They will not return for about seven moons." Her features hardened as she said, "Soldier coats from your fort came in here this morning. They brought two of our elderly warriors into the village, dead. The lieutenant said Spotted Tail and Short Bear had murdered one of his soldiers.

"Other aged men here in our village told him the old warriors would not murder anyone. The lieutenant became very angry and started shooting. His men started shooting, too. They killed old men and old women—ten of them. They shot my mother, White Wing, but she is still alive. They did not see Curly and me, or they would have shot us, too. The white man you saw stopped this morning to help us. He has saved my mother's life."

Theron Tyler's face went bleak as stone. He looked at Brooke, then glanced at his men, who had heard every word. Each knew what the other was thinking...*Dolan.*

Tyler turned back to Gentle Fawn. "Ma'am, could you describe this lieutenant for me? I assume you saw him."

"I saw him," she said. "A name would be better than a description, would it not?"

"It sure would."

"I heard one of his men call him Lieutenant Dolan."

To Brooke, Tyler said, "Dolan and his bunch are from Missouri. Dragoons. They've been accused of this sort of thing before, but there's never been any proof."

"There is now," Brooke said.

Tyler turned back to Gentle Fawn. "Ma'am, this sort of conduct is inexcusable for men of our army. I assure you that Lieutenant Dolan and his men will face charges for what they did."

Curly's anger exploded. "I want to kill them! Especially that lieutenant! He is a coward! Only a coward would kill old people who can do him no harm!"

"I agree with you, son," Tyler said. "Believe me, they will pay for what they've done."

"Will they die?"

Tyler ran a hand over his mouth. "I can't say, son, but this will be reported to our chief at the fort, and they will be dealt with severely."

It was clear by the look in Curly's eyes that he didn't believe the soldier coats would punish their own men.

"We would like to meet this white man who saved your mother's life, Gentle Fawn," Tyler said. "Is it someone you and your people know?"

"Not until today, Major. He came here at just the right time this morning to help deliver my baby. We both would have died if it were not for him."

"You just gave birth to a baby? You shouldn't be standing here talking to us. You must go to your teepee and lie down."

Even as Tyler spoke, a whirling dizziness overcame Gentle Fawn and she started to fall. Curly lost his grip on her, and Tyler quickly moved to catch her.

Andrea wanted to help and was being lifted from the wagon by Benny Walker. Marian Brooke had the same idea, and drew alongside Andrea, saying, "I'll see to her, honey."

"I'll go with you," Andrea insisted.

Both women walked up just as Theron looked in their direction, steadying Gentle Fawn. She had not passed out, but was very pale, and her eyes were dull.

"Theron, did I hear right?" Andrea asked. "She just had a baby this morning?"

"Yes."

Andrea turned to the boy and said, "Your name is Curly, right?"

Curly nodded.

"Curly, which tent is Gentle Fawn's? We need to lay her down."

Curly pointed to the teepee. "That one. Our mother is there, and my new little nephew, Quiet Thunder."

Captain Bernard Trent's wife, Lily, rushed up. "Can I help, too?"

Curly darted to the teepee and went inside, and the three women and the major headed that way.

Brooke turned to his officers and Tyler's unit. "Men, you heard it from Gentle Fawn's own mouth. Some soldiers from Fort Clark came in here this morning and shot down a bunch of old men and women. The rest of the tribe is out on a buffalo hunt. Go tell everybody else in the wagons so they'll know what's going on. We'll pull out once we know everything's under control."

While the soldiers, women, and children were climbing out of the wagons to stretch their legs, Curly bolted out of the teepee again.

"Gentle Fawn! John Stranger is gone! Mother thought he was coming to join us."

Tyler stopped, allowing Gentle Fawn to speak. She tried to focus her eyes on her brother's face. "He must be close by, Curly," she said. "He is probably watering his horse."

"I will go see!" Curly ran toward the east edge of the village.

"Let's get her inside," Marian said.

Tyler eased Gentle Fawn down beside her mother, who was studying the faces of the soldier and the three women. Gentle Fawn managed a brief explanation of why the army wagon train had come into the village, and White Wing smiled.

Marian spied the water pail and came back with a cup of water for Gentle Fawn. "Here, dear, drink this."

Young Curly ran as hard as he could and skidded to a halt when he came upon the spot where Stranger had ground-reined his horse.

"No, John Stranger!" he cried. "You have not left us yet! Where are you?"

Even as he spoke, Curly made a dash for the ravine, running his eyes in three directions. He could not see Stranger anywhere. He stopped at the rim and searched it both ways. His heart sank. The only white man he had ever trusted was gone.

Gentle Fawn drained the cup and handed it back to Marian. "What is your name, kind lady?"

"Marian Brooke. I am wife of Lieutenant Colonel George Brooke, who is leading the wagon train to Fort Clark."

Gentle Fawn fixed her gaze on the other two women.

The captain's wife said, "I am Lily Trent, Gentle Fawn. My husband is Captain Bernard Trent."

"And I am Andrea Tyler, Major Tyler's wife."

Gentle Fawn looked more closely at Andrea. "You will soon deliver a child, Mrs. Tyler?"

"Yes."

"I am sorry I cannot offer you a chair to sit in."

"That's all right," Andrea said. "The main thing is to get you comfortable. I'll sit when I return to my wagon."

"Gentle Fawn," the major said, "did I hear correctly? The name of the man who came here this morning is John *Stranger?*"

"Yes."

"I sure hope I get to meet him," Tyler said. "Is he a doctor of some kind?"

"No. He removed a bullet from my mother's chest, sewed

up the wound, and bandaged it, and he saved my life and my baby's, but he is not a doctor. Curly and I believe he is an angel, like those spoken of in the white man's Bible, though John Stranger told us he is not."

Curly plunged through the teepee opening. "Gentle Fawn! John Stranger's horse is not there! He has gone!"

Gentle Fawn frowned. "I am sorry for that. I wanted to thank him once again and tell him goodbye. He did tell us he had to hurry to help some people in Wyoming's mountains."

Little Quiet Thunder woke up and began to cry.

"You stay right there, Gentle Fawn," Lily Trent said. "I'll get him for you."

Gentle Fawn watched Lily's every move as she went to the baby. Something shiny next to the crib caught her eye. As Lily eased the baby into her arms, she pointed with her chin. "Curly, what is that? The object that shines."

Curly picked up the round object and held it in the flat of his palm.

"May I see it?" Tyler said.

Curly placed it in his hand.

"I thought at first it was a silver dollar," the major said, "but it's some kind of medallion. There's a raised five-point star in the center, and around its curved edge there is Scripture."

"John Stranger left it, I am sure," Gentle Fawn said. "What does it say?"

Tyler eyed it appreciatively. "Well, it sure does make your Mr. Stranger seem like an angel. Here," he said, handing the medallion to Gentle Fawn, "read it so we can all hear."

Gentle Fawn silently read the inscription. A smile curved her lips. She looked at the army women and then at her mother. "It says, *'THE STRANGER THAT SHALL COME FROM A FAR LAND.'* Then in small letters, 'Deuteronomy 29:22.'"

"From a far land," Curly said. "From *what* far land, my sister?"

"Maybe where he came from and what he is must be kept a

secret. Even as the piece of silver says, he is the stranger from a far country, but it does not say *what* country."

Theron Tyler looked at his wife, then the other women, and hunched his broad shoulders. "I don't know what to think, but one thing's for sure, the man came along just in time."

"Do angels ride horses?" Curly asked.

Gentle Fawn's eyes welled up with tears as she looked toward the sky. "Thank you, Sky Father, for sending John Stranger." Then, closing her eyes, she gripped the medallion to her heart. "The Sky Father bless you, John Stranger. I will never forget you. And I will see that Quiet Thunder knows who you are and what you did for us. He will never forget your name. I promise."

Still trying not to let on that she was in pain, Andrea Tyler turned to her husband. "Theron, can we take these three to the fort so they can be cared for until their people return?"

"Yes, I'm sure Colonel Lawson would welcome them."

"Good. The army doctor can give White Wing proper care, and he can give mother and baby thorough examinations to make sure they're all right."

Gentle Fawn smiled up at Andrea Tyler. She was beginning to feel a kinship with this woman.

Curly felt differently. "Gentle Fawn," he said, "I know these people mean well, but I do not want to go to their fort. That is where the soldier coats are who killed the old people and shot our mother. When they see our mother, they will recognize her. They will shoot all of us, even little Quiet Thunder."

Major Tyler looked at Curly with steady eyes. "Curly, you need not fear Lieutenant Dolan or his men. They are going to be punished for what they did. They will be in no position to harm any of you."

"But I do not want to go where the evil lieutenant is. I hate him. You will not be able to stop him from shooting us."

Andrea moved to Curly and laid a tender hand on his shoulder. "Curly, you can trust my husband. What he is telling you is true.

He is a major. Do you understand? His rank is higher than the lieutenant's. Nothing bad is going to happen to any of you at the fort."

Curly did not reply, but stubbornness shone in his dark eyes.

Andrea pressed further. "Your mother needs the care of the fort's doctor. So does your sister and her baby. All army people are not bad like the lieutenant and his men."

"But I do not want to be where they are unless I can kill them. I would be happy to do that. But I am just one boy. There are too many of them."

"Son," White Wing said, "these people are trying to help us. I believe the major speaks the truth. He will not allow the evil lieutenant to harm us."

Andrea's hand was still on Curly's shoulder when she felt a wrenching in her midsection and doubled over.

"Andrea!" Theron moved toward her and placed an arm around her. "Is it—?"

"Yes. It's time. *Right now!*"

"There is another pallet over there," Gentle Fawn said, sitting up with the baby in her arms and pointing across the teepee.

Theron helped his wife to the pallet and eased her down. Another pain hit. As she moaned, Marian and Lily moved in close.

"Major," Marian said, "it would be best if you and Curly step outside. Lily and I will take care of the delivery."

"Okay. We'll be just outside. If you need me, you holler, y'hear?"

"I can holler loud," Marian said and smiled. "Just go ask my husband. Now, git!"

The sun was sinking past the horizon when the cry of a newborn baby filled the air.

Theron Tyler waited, each minute seeming like an eternity.

He heard the sound of unintelligible conversation inside the teepee and could stand it no longer. "Hey!" he called, taking a couple of steps toward the closed flap. "Is everything all right in there?"

"Mother and baby are fine!" came Lily Trent's voice. "Just a couple of minutes!"

Tyler scrubbed a nervous hand over his face and looked at Brooke and Trent. "I didn't know a man could get so tight inside. Nothing I faced in the Mexican War gave me anything like this."

"It's good for you," Brooke said with a chuckle. "It'll make you appreciate your little one even more."

"Well, my little *what*, sir? I want to know if it's a boy or a g—"

"You can come in now, Major," Lily said, throwing back the flap.

Andrea lay on a pallet with a tiny bundle in her arms. She looked pale, but her smile was brilliant. The women looked on as the major knelt down, alternating his gaze from his wife's face to the tiny face in the blanket.

Andrea's smile widened. "Daddy, say hello to your son. Thann, this is your daddy."

Theron's eyes filled with tears. "*Thann!* I have a son!" He bent down and kissed his wife, then kissed his little boy.

Gentle Fawn, who also held her little boy in a blanket, was feeling even more kinship with Andrea Tyler. "This makes me very happy, Major," she said. "Your little Thann Tyler has come into the world on the same day as my little Quiet Thunder."

CHAPTER

TWELVE

———— ◆ ————

It was almost noon the next day when the army wagon train arrived at Fort Clark.

The corporal in charge of the gate directed two troopers to open the gate wide and then stepped out to greet the two front riders. "Welcome back, Major Tyler. I assume this is Lieutenant Colonel Brooke?"

"Yes. Colonel Brooke, this is Corporal Clifford Warrick."

"Corporal." Brooke nodded.

"Welcome to Fort Clark, Colonel," Warrick said. Then to Tyler, "Major, how is your wife?"

"She's well, Cliff. Just yesterday she gave birth to our healthy baby boy!"

"Well, congratulations, sir! And how is the father doing?"

"Wonderful, thank you. Would you tell Dr. Hoffman that we need his help. I'd like him to check my wife and son, just to make sure everything's all right. And we have some Indians from Gray Shadow's village with us. A young Oglala mother had her first baby yesterday too, and we have her mother, a middle-aged woman with a bullet wound."

"I'll go and tell him right now, sir," Warrick said, and hurried away to the infirmary.

To the troopers who held the gate, Tyler said, "Colonel Lawson will want to know we are here. Will one of you advise him? Explain that we must go to the infirmary before we meet with him."

"The colonel isn't here right now, Major. He'll be returning at about two o'clock this afternoon."

"All right. When he arrives, please advise him that Lieutenant Colonel Brooke and the wagon train from Illinois are here."

"Yes, sir."

By the time the lead wagon rolled through the gate, a crowd of soldiers, plus women and children, were waiting to greet them.

Lieutenant Dolan and his dragoons stayed in the background.

Dr. Wendell Hoffman was in his late fifties and had served as an army surgeon in the Mexican War. He was deeply respected by the men and women of Fort Clark.

When Hoffman finally stepped out onto the infirmary porch and said, "You gentlemen may come in now. I'm finished with the examinations," Theron Tyler realized how tightly he'd been clenching his teeth.

"Is my mother all right, Doctor?" Curly asked.

"It will take her a good deal of time to recover, son, but she's doing fine."

"And my sister and my nephew are all right?"

"They certainly are," the silver-haired physician said with a smile.

"Then I will wait out here."

"Fine. We'll be assigning you and your family a place to stay in just a little while."

Curly nodded, his eyes searching the grounds for Lieutenant Dolan.

Dolan stood near one of the warehouses with Sergeant Cahill and Corporal Whitman. The front of the infirmary was barely visible from where they stood.

"We should've made sure that stinkin' Indian woman was dead before we left the village," he said.

"What I'm wondering," Whitman said, "is how come we didn't find that kid and the woman with the baby when we searched the teepees."

"They must've been hiding out somewhere," Cahill said. "So what're we going to do now?"

Dolan spit in the dust. "Nothin'. No doubt they've told Tyler and Brooke what happened. But it's our word against theirs, and they're nothin' but filthy redskins. Lawson isn't goin' to listen to them."

"I sure hope not. The woman who threw the rock can identify us, even if the other woman and the kid can't."

Dolan spit again. "Don't worry your gizzard about her, Lenny. No scummy Indian is goin' to get us into trouble."

At the infirmary, Lily Trent and Marian Brooke were seated on wooden chairs beside the cots holding White Wing, Gentle Fawn, and Andrea Tyler. Both babies were asleep in cribs next to their mothers.

"I've got them resting for the moment," Hoffman said to Major Tyler and Colonel Brooke. "Sit down, gentlemen."

Theron picked up a chair and placed it next to Andrea's cot. Brooke sat next to his wife.

"Major Tyler," the doctor said, "everything is fine. These women did a beautiful job in delivering little Thann and caring for your wife."

Theron smiled at Lily and Marian. "Thank you, ladies."

"Gentle Fawn here has told me what happened at the village and about the mysterious man named John Stranger," Hoffman continued. "I've examined Gentle Fawn, little Quiet Thunder, and White Wing. I have to say that this Stranger fella knew what he was doing."

"He was an angel, Dr. Hoffman," Gentle Fawn said.

Hoffman gave her a placating grin.

Sounds from outside drew Tyler's attention and he went to check. "The colonel's back," he reported.

"We'll give him a few minutes, then head for his office," Brooke said.

Tyler nodded and returned to Andrea. "You'll like our apartment, honey," he said, stroking her cheek. "And so will Thann."

"I'm sure we will," she said softly. "The best part about it is we'll be together."

"I like the sound of that, Mrs. Tyler."

Corporal Warrick had met Colonel Lawson and Lieutenant Thompson before they passed through the gate and informed them that Lieutenant Colonel Brooke and the remainder of the Fifth Infantry had arrived, along with the officers' wives and children. He also mentioned the Indian guests who were now at the infirmary.

Curly was still sitting outside the infirmary door scrutinizing every soldier that passed by. As the newly arrived column filed in and the men of the fort gathered to welcome their commandant, Curly's keen eyes caught sight of Lieutenant Dolan. He was standing with two other soldiers Curly recognized.

Dolan, Cahill, and Wylie Odoms heard Colonel Lawson ask Corporal Warrick to fetch Brooke and Tyler to his office.

"I hope Lawson's got the good sense to shrug off anything

those Indians have told Brooke and Tyler," Wylie said.

Dolan chuckled and was about to comment when he heard a screeching, high-pitched "Hokahey-y!" an instant before a ninety-pound body leaped on his back.

Curly yelled the war cry again and dug his fingernails across Dolan's eyes. He clung like a leech, and even as Odoms and Cahill tried to pull him loose, Dolan fell facedown with Curly still on him. It took all three soldiers to pull the boy loose.

The crowd pressed in, and Colonel Lawson looked on from astride his mount as Dolan rose to his feet, cursing and rubbing his burning eyes.

Curly was being held spread-eagle, and Dolan was yelling, "I'll kill 'im! I'll kill 'im!" when Tyler and Brooke arrived on the scene.

"Curly," Tyler said, "let me handle this. The men will let go if you promise me you'll settle down."

The boy relaxed. At least he had done some damage to Dolan. It would satisfy him for the moment. "I will fight them no more, Major," Curly said.

By this time, Colonel Lawson was off his horse. Curly stood next to Tyler and looked at Dolan with fiery eyes.

Dolan met Curly's gaze and hissed, "Stinkin' Indian! I don't care if you are just a kid, I'd kill you if I had half a chance!"

"You are a low-belly coward!" Curly spat back. "You kill old men and women! I grow up, I kill *you!*"

"What's going on here?" Lawson demanded.

"Colonel Brooke and I will explain it all as soon as we can meet with you in your office, sir," Tyler said.

"All right, Major," Lawson said. "Let's break it up. Everybody back to your duties." He turned to Brooke and offered his hand. "Welcome Colonel Brooke. We'll meet in my office immediately."

Lawson then turned to Dolan. "Lieutenant, it appears this young Indian knows you. He's too young to be a warrior, so you couldn't have met him on the battlefield."

"I'll explain that to you, sir," Tyler said. "And I request that you command Lieutenant Dolan and all the men who were on patrol with him yesterday to appear at your office thirty minutes after you meet with Lieutenant Colonel Brooke and myself."

"Then so be it," Lawson said. "Lieutenant Dolan, you and your patrol assemble before my office in half an hour."

"Yes, sir," Dolan said, still blinking and wiping at his eyes.

Thirty minutes after the command had been given, Lieutenant Dolan and his men stood at attention in front of the colonel's office. Colonel Lawson emerged from the office, his features grim. Brooke and Tyler followed. The dragoons saw two soldiers carry White Wing on a stretcher, with Gentle Fawn walking alongside her.

"Lieutenant Dolan," Lawson said, "Colonel Brooke and Major Tyler have given me information that I find very unpleasant. It seems there was blood shed yesterday by you and your patrol at the Oglala village ten miles south of here."

The dragoons stood erect, shoulders back, heads level.

"May I speak, sir?" Dolan said.

"Not yet."

White Wing's stretcher was laid on the porch in the shade, and a chair was brought from inside for Gentle Fawn. Lily Trent was taking care of Quiet Thunder in the infirmary. Curly and a trooper remained inside the colonel's office at Lawson's command.

When Gentle Fawn had been seated, Lawson ran his gaze over the faces of the dragoons and said, "Major Tyler tells me that two elderly warriors of the Oglala village were killed by your men, apparently at Point Nemaha yesterday."

"That's right, sir," Dolan said, "but only after they had murdered Jim Pollard. When we arrived back here late yesterday afternoon, I told you two warriors had shot him for no apparent reason, other than plain old Indian meanness."

"I know what you told me, Dolan," Lawson said, "and I believed you. But now I'm having a problem. Trooper Pollard's body was already in the coffin when it was brought to the burial service this morning. I was told by one of the men who rode with me today that he had seen the body, and there was only one bullet hole in it. Smack in the middle of the forehead. Correct?"

"Yes, sir," Dolan said.

"You told me both warriors killed him. Are you saying they were such good shots that they both put bullets in the exact same spot?"

"Well…uh, sir, what I really didn't have time to explain was that both of them shot at Pollard, but only one of them hit him. We opened fire on both of them for that reason."

"I see. And I assume you really didn't have time to mention that they were old men—not strong, youthful warriors."

Dolan swallowed hard. "That's it, sir."

"I've learned from Major Tyler and Lieutenant Colonel Brooke that ten elderly Oglala men and women were shot down by you and your patrol yesterday at the village."

Lawson turned to Tyler. "Major, you told me that Gentle Fawn here identified Lieutenant Dolan as the man who led in the murders at the village yesterday. Would you explain how she did that?"

"I'll let her answer for herself, sir." He turned to look at Gentle Fawn and said, "Tell us how you know it was this man, Gentle Fawn."

"Because I saw him, and I learned his name when one of his men called him Lieutenant Dolan. I told Major Tyler his name yesterday." She pointed to Dolan. "And that is him. I also recognize those men with him."

"Colonel, this woman's lying! She wasn't even there! Sure, we shot those Indians, but only when the men picked up rifles to cut us down."

"You mean there were some warriors in the village, Lieutenant?" Tyler said. "*Young* warriors?"

"Well…no. But an old man can kill you just as dead as a young man. We had no choice. Right men?"

"Right!" came a chorus of voices.

"See, Colonel? My men—"

"Just a moment, Dolan," Lawson said. "Major Tyler, would you speak to the victim who survived yesterday's shooting? Let's hear from her."

Tyler went to help White Wing sit up and asked her to tell the story exactly as it happened. White Wing spoke weakly, but told how Lieutenant Dolan fired on the elderly Indians before the old men could even get to some spears to defend themselves. The old women were cut down, too. She then told how she retaliated by throwing a rock at the lieutenant, and one of the troopers shot her.

"She's lying, Colonel!" Dolan shouted. "Those old warriors went for rifles that were right close by! We had no choice but to shoot them. It was them or us!"

"*You* lie!" Gentle Fawn said. "They had only spears! But they did not try to use them until the lieutenant had already opened fire!"

"You weren't even there to see us! You got my name from the lying old squaw…and you're only goin' by what she told you!"

Anger reddened Gentle Fawn's features. "I *was* there, Lieutenant! My brother and I were in my teepee, and we saw it all! We ran and hid in the ravine when my mother threw the rock at you and was shot down. We saw your men going through all the teepees, but we stayed hidden because you would have killed us, too." She looked around and said, "Where is my brother, Major Tyler? Let him come and tell what he saw."

Lawson spoke up. "I have ordered your brother held in my office because of his age, ma'am." Then he set hard eyes on Dolan. "Now I know when and where the boy met you, and why he attacked you, Lieutenant. It is quite evident that you and your men shot those Indians."

"Yes, sir, we did, but in self-defense! These Indians lie! Right, men?"

Again the dragoons agreed.

Lawson drew in a deep breath and let it out slowly. "Lieutenant Dolan, why were the old women killed? Only White Wing threw a rock at you, correct?"

"She's the only one who threw a rock, sir, yes. But when we were shooting it out with the warriors, the women just got caught in the crossfire. It couldn't be helped."

"Again you lie!" Gentle Fawn said. "You shot them yourself, and emptied your gun. But some of them were not dead. You then told your men to finish them off!"

A pleading look etched itself on Dolan's face. "Colonel Lawson, you're not going to take the word of lying Indians over that of your own men, are you?"

Lawson was considering his answer when Tyler said, "May I remind you, Colonel, that this is not the first, second, third, or even fourth time that charges of this same kind of conduct have been leveled at Lieutenant Dolan and these men. Since we had no proof, we had to take their word for it. But how many times do we have to hear the same whistle before we realize it's blowing?"

All eyes were riveted on the commandant.

Lawson rubbed his chin and spoke. "I find myself between a rock and a hard place. That Oglalas were shot and killed yesterday by the dragoons, there is no question. Even they have admitted it. What it boils down to is Lieutenant Dolan's word—and that of his men—against the word of these women and the boy. The Indians say it was murder. The soldiers say it was self-defense. There is no concrete proof either way."

Lawson took a deep breath. "If I had concrete evidence that there was murder involved, I would sentence every one of you men in this unit to the firing squad. However, since we lack that evidence, I cannot do it. However, since this kind of charge has come to my ears repeatedly about you men, you are hereby

dishonorably discharged from the United States Army. You will
surrender your weapons immediately."

Dolan's back arched in stunned disbelief and he started to
protest.

Several soldiers had moved in silently behind the dragoons
by a prearranged signal from the commandant. Dolan froze when
he heard more than a dozen hammers cocked.

"You will each drop your weapons right now," Lawson said,
"and you will turn in your uniforms within thirty minutes. You all
have civilian work clothes. You will leave this fort on foot immediately after you turn in your uniforms.

"One more thing. I want it understood that I believe Gentle
Fawn and White Wing. Yes, and the boy. I simply cannot make
myself believe that a handful of elderly Sioux warriors would be so
foolish as to take on an entire unit of professional soldiers. I feel certain that some of you men did not obey your lieutenant and fire on
the aged Indians. However, since not one of you came forth to report,
you must take the consequences with the rest of them. That is all."

A half-hour later, Curly stood between his sister and Major
Tyler and watched as the dishonored ex-soldiers walked out of the
fort, some with their heads hung low. Bill Dolan matched Curly's
hate-filled glare with one of his own.

During the next seven days, White Wing was kept under Dr.
Hoffman's watchful eye. Gentle Fawn, her baby, and her brother
were given quarters in the same building as the Tylers, and Andrea
and Gentle Fawn spent a lot of time together with their babies.

On the eighth day after they had left, Gray Shadow and his people
returned to the village to find the twelve bodies on scaffolds. The

rains had washed away any evidence of horses with iron shoes, but since White Wing, Gentle Fawn, and Curly were not among the dead, Gray Shadow assumed the soldier coats had captured them and taken them to Fort Clark.

The Oglalas were mystified as to who had placed the bodies on the scaffolds. Certainly the soldiers would not have done it. And White Wing and Curly were not strong enough to have done it. Being great with child, Gentle Fawn could not have helped.

Gray Shadow, seething with wrath, led his warriors out of the village, galloping hard for the fort.

Trooper Gene Sellers, on duty in the watchtower, spotted the Oglalas. "Corporal Warrick! Indians coming from due south!"

Warrick and two other troopers peered through a narrow opening in the stockade wall. "How many?"

"Better than two hundred is my guess!"

"Sound the alarm!"

The clear tones of a bugle split the air, and soldiers came running from all over the compound for their assigned places on the banquette.

The women and children hurried to their quarters.

Colonel Lawson, Lieutenant Colonel Brooke, and Major Tyler drew up to the partially opened gate to view the oncoming Sioux who were still a good three miles away.

"Colonel Lawson!" Trooper Sellers shouted. "They're coming under a white flag!"

Lawson waved that he understood, then peered at the approaching Indians through his binoculars. It took only a second to see the flag. "He's right," Lawson said. "They probably just returned from their buffalo hunt and found those bodies you told me about. Let's get Gentle Fawn out here."

The Oglalas drew up about a hundred yards from the front

gate and sat on their horses in a straight line. A few of their leaders urged their horses forward and approached the fort. Gentle Fawn was ready to meet them just inside the gate with Theron Tyler.

"All right, Gentle Fawn," Lawson said, "let's you and me move out together so they can see us. Colonel Brooke and Major Tyler, you come with us."

Gentle Fawn raised a hand and waved as they moved forward a few steps. The instant Fire Eagle saw Gentle Fawn, the fierce look on his face disappeared. He slid from his pinto's back and saw immediately that his squaw was no longer with child.

"The baby?" he said, taking Gentle Fawn in his arms.

"Oh, my love, everything is fine. You have a healthy little son!"

Fire Eagle raised his hands toward the Sky Father, then turned and told Gray Shadow and Laughing Horse they had a new grandson. Though neither smiled, a gentle look came into their eyes.

Colonel Lawson raised his right hand in a sign of peace, and said, "Chief Gray Shadow, please dismount. You and your men are welcome. White Wing, Curly, and Fire Eagle's son are inside. Come."

The colonel led them through the gate with Gentle Fawn at her husband's side. Gentle Fawn began to explain what had happened.

At the infirmary, Laughing Horse found his squaw alive but weak. Dr. Hoffman explained that White Wing had been wounded seriously, but that she would regain her health. Laughing Horse was relieved to know that Curly had not been harmed.

Marian Brooke came in at that moment, carrying little Quiet Thunder. Fire Eagle took him in his arms and seemed exceedingly pleased with the baby's name.

Colonel Lawson then took Gray Shadow and Fire Eagle, along with Brooke and Tyler, to his office. Lawson asked Major Tyler to explain what Lieutenant Dolan and his men had done.

Gray Shadow and Fire Eagle were partially pacified when they learned of the dragoons' dishonorable discharge from the army and their expulsion from the fort.

Dr. Hoffman provided medicine and bandages for White Wing, and Colonel Lawson offered to have her and the others transported to the village in an army wagon, which Gray Shadow accepted.

The wagon was brought, and as Fire Eagle was about to lift his wife into it, Andrea Tyler embraced her. They held onto each other for a long moment.

"Gentle Fawn," Andrea said, with tears shining in her eyes, "it is my wish that since our sons were born on the same day and at the same place, they will eventually know each other and be friends. As we are friends."

"This I would love to see," Gentle Fawn said with a smile. "Please come to visit me at the village. I will welcome you."

Andrea held onto her husband's arm as the wagon passed through the gate with Gray Shadow, Laughing Horse, and Fire Eagle just ahead of it. Soon they reached the long line of Oglala warriors and headed across the plain. Before they passed from view, Gentle Fawn turned and waved to Andrea.

That night, as Fire Eagle and Gentle Fawn lay side by side with little Quiet Thunder asleep in his crib, Gentle Fawn said, "My husband, there is much to tell you. We have not had a moment for me to explain that if it were not for a man named John Stranger, your son and I would be dead, and so would my mother."

"Please tell me," he said, holding her hand.

While the night breeze softly brushed against the sides of the teepee and the crickets sang to a full moon, Gentle Fawn told her husband how the mysterious man had delivered the baby, and why she had named their son Quiet Thunder. She added that it was John Stranger who saved White Wing's life by skillfully removing the bullet from her chest.

The moon's bright beams illumined the teepee with a soft silver light as Gentle Fawn sat up for a moment, reached for a pouch, and pulled out the medallion. She handed it to Fire Eagle, who turned it about in his fingers. Since it was not light enough for him to read the inscription, Gentle Fawn told him what it said.

"Fire Eagle would like to one day meet this stranger from a far land. He would like to thank him for what he did for his squaw and little son...and for White Wing."

"Perhaps the Sky Father will allow that," Gentle Fawn said. She thought about the Sioux custom for young boys. When they turned sixteen, they would go out with bow and arrow to make their first kill of a wild animal. The right paw of the animal would be strung on a leather thong and worn around the boy's neck for the rest of his life.

As Fire Eagle placed the medallion back in her hand, Gentle Fawn said, "I will keep this. When our Quiet Thunder is sixteen grasses and it is time for his first kill, he will wear the medallion on the thong along with the paw. I want him to always remember the name of John Stranger, who saved his life on that rainy, thunder-filled day."

CHAPTER

THIRTEEN

During the next two years, Indians and whites in Nebraska Territory lived peaceably. Gentle Fawn and Andrea Tyler visited each other often, and their friendship deepened. Quiet Thunder and Thann Tyler became playmates.

There was a sad time in the Oglala village in late October 1855, when Gray Shadow's squaw, Little Flower, died of a prolonged fever.

On November 2, Major Tyler was summoned to Colonel Lawson's office. The sky was heavy with clouds, and little flakes of snow were riding the wind.

Lawson looked up and smiled. "Looks like we're going to have some weather."

"Yes, sir. The wrong kind. Sergeant Garrison said you wanted to see me, sir."

"Yes. Take off your coat and hat and sit down."

Lawson held up an official-looking sheet of paper. "Major, I have a letter here from Washington. You have just been promoted to Lieutenant Colonel, and you're being transferred to Fort Pierre, Dakota Territory."

"How did this come about, sir?"

Lawson leaned forward on his elbows. "You're aware that Colonel Abermarle Cady is commandant at Fort Pierre."

"Yes, sir. We fought together in the Mexican War. He was my commanding officer when I was a lieutenant."

"Well, Colonel Cady wrote Washington asking to have you transferred there. The Sioux in Dakota Territory are getting harder to handle. Cady told Washington he needed you as second in command at Pierre, so his request was granted. He then told them he would only accept your transfer if they made you lieutenant colonel."

Tyler grinned. "Bless him."

"There's an army wagon train coming through Point Nemaha in about a week. They'll be stopping here before heading north, and you and your family can join the train when they move on. I'm sure you'll get to Fort Pierre before heavy snow."

On November 8, Sub-Chief Fire Eagle, dressed in heavy buckskins, was crossing the village under a clear, cold sky when he heard some of the women chattering and pointing westward. An army wagon was coming toward the village, escorted by a dozen riders. A white flag flapped in the breeze.

Fire Eagle smiled. No doubt Andrea Tyler was bringing little Thann for another visit. It had been a few weeks since the two women had been together. Gentle Fawn would be glad to see Andrea again.

By the time the wagon rolled into the village, some of the Oglala women had alerted Gentle Fawn, who now stood beside her husband. They were surprised to see Andrea's husband on the front seat beside the driver. The major had never come with Andrea and his son for a visit.

Theron Tyler smiled at them, jumped out, and hurried to

the rear of the wagon to help Andrea and Thann down.

Gentle Fawn moved forward and embraced Andrea. "It is good to see you. Do I see sadness in your face?"

"Yes. May we go to your teepee and talk?"

Inside, there was a small fire burning, and the air was warm. White Wing and Quiet Thunder joyfully greeted them, and soon the boys were busy at play.

Andrea looked at both women with sad eyes. "We're being transferred to Fort Pierre in Dakota Territory."

"Fort Pierre," White Wing said. "Our people are doing much fighting with the soldier coats in Dakota Territory."

Andrea nodded. "That's why my husband is being transferred. He's been promoted to lieutenant colonel and will be second in command at the fort."

Tears glistened in Gentle Fawn's eyes. "You are on your way now?"

"Yes."

"My heart is in the ground, Andrea."

"So is mine."

"We will never see you again?" White Wing asked.

"I don't know."

Gentle Fawn put her arms around her friend. "My heart will stay in the ground until I see you again, Andrea. This Oglala friend loves you very much."

"And I love you, Gentle Fawn. And I love White Wing and little Quiet Thunder."

The women reminisced while the boys played, giggling and squealing. After about half an hour Andrea called to Thann. "I hate to do this, my friends, but I must go." She embraced White Wing and then turned to Gentle Fawn.

"We will not say goodbye, Andrea," Gentle Fawn said. "We will just say, 'Until we meet again.'"

Andrea turned and picked up Thann and moved to the teepee opening. Gentle Fawn threw on her buffalo hide coat to go outside. She watched as Andrea's husband helped his family into the wagon.

Andrea sat looking out the rear opening, and as the wagon started to pull away, she forced a smile. "Until we meet again, Gentle Fawn," she said.

"Until we meet again, my friend."

There was much excitement in Gray Shadow's Oglala village on a hot August day in 1856. Laughing Horse and White Wing stood with Gentle Fawn and little three-year-old Quiet Thunder as the hunting party returned at sunset. Many of the Oglalas stood with them.

Curly had turned sixteen grasses the day before. Fire Eagle and several warriors had taken him out this morning, and now he was returning with a wild boar. Curly had made his first kill.

The crowd cheered as Curly beamed with pride. The boar was skinned out and the right front hoof cut off before the carcass was put on a spit over crackling flames.

While the hog was cooking, along with several chunks of buffalo meat, a special ceremony was held. Curly's father, Laughing Horse, placed a leather thong over his son's head. On the thong was the tip of the boar's hoof Curly would wear for the rest of his life. He was now a mighty hunter.

While the Oglalas cheered, Curly dreamed of the day he would become a mighty warrior.

In September, Colonel Lawson was transferred to a fort in Arizona, and Lieutenant Colonel George Brooke was made a full colonel and sent back to Fort Abraham Lincoln as its commandant.

Colonel Ronald Swager, who had been second in command

at a fort in Kansas, became commandant of Fort Clark. Swager was young and eager to make a name for himself. He believed he would bring the Indians in Nebraska Territory into subjection with an iron hand. Swager so infuriated the Indians by his harsh and cruel ways that some of the chiefs held a powwow and decided he had to be eliminated.

On a brisk day in late October, Fire Eagle and sub-chiefs from Cheyenne, Arapaho, and Blackfeet tribes lay in wait for the colonel and a unit of fifteen men who were returning to the fort from Point Nemaha. Scouts had seen them pass through the area earlier that morning.

Halfway to Chief Gray Shadow's Oglala village, the army unit was ambushed and wiped out.

The next day, a Fort Clark patrol rode south in search of the missing commandant and his unit. They came upon the slaughtered soldiers. Swager had been staked to the ground and skinned alive.

A new commandant was sent to Fort Clark who unleashed a series of attacks on Sioux, Cheyenne, Arapaho, and Blackfeet villages. The Nebraska plains, which had known relative peace for over three years, were once again soaked with blood.

Hungry Bear, an Oglala chief from Wyoming, brought his tribe to Nebraska and joined Gray Shadow's tribe, beefing up the number of warriors to fight the army. Gray Shadow, who was ten years older than Hungry Bear, became chief of the combined tribes.

Fire Eagle proved himself a fierce and rugged warrior. In the heat of battle, he had shown himself unafraid of the educated officers and highly trained troopers, and was undaunted by the army's better weapons. His warriors revered him as a fighting leader and went with him into battle with tenacity.

Fire Eagle's fame spread among the U.S. army troops, and with it the trepidation they felt when there was a possibility they would fight him.

Another warrior gaining in stature was young Red Cloud, now in his early twenties. As second to Fire Eagle in prowess and fighting ability, Red Cloud assisted the sub-chief in training prospective young warriors.

When Curly turned eighteen grasses, he could formally begin his training. He decided he couldn't wait that long and approached Fire Eagle to begin teaching him now. Fire Eagle sensed the latent heart of a great warrior in his young brother-in-law and began training him privately. When he was too busy, he had Red Cloud do it.

Curly caught on to hand-to-hand fighting quickly, and he learned how to throw a spear and use bow and arrow accurately in battle conditions, even from the back of a running horse. He also learned how to swing low on one side of a galloping pinto, using the horse as a shield, and fire a musket one-handed with precision from underneath its neck. The eager youth was also picking up skill with the tomahawk.

When Curly turned eighteen, he was already as prepared as he would ever be for his first battle.

Curly approached Fire Eagle and asked him to obtain Chief Gray Shadow's permission to fight in the next battle. Gray Shadow agreed. Laughing Horse was exceedingly proud that his son was considered ready to fight in battle and gave his permission.

Laughing Horse's confidence was not shared by his squaw, White Wing. She thought her son still too young to go up against seasoned warriors, but Sioux mothers had no say in such matters.

Five-year-old Quiet Thunder had spent a great deal of time at the practice field, observing his Uncle Curly. At sunset on a particularly hot day in late August, Quiet Thunder left the field after watching Red Cloud and Curly work together, and ran to his teepee, where his mother was stirring small chunks of squirrel meat in a kettle.

Fire Eagle, about to enter the teepee, overhead his little son saying, "—just like Father."

Gentle Fawn smiled at her husband, asking if there had been any trouble with the soldier coats today.

"We only saw one patrol at a great distance. They did not seem to notice us."

"Father, it is time to put me up on your shoulders," Quiet Thunder said, lifting his arms up.

Fire Eagle dropped to one knee and looked the boy in the eye. "In a moment," he said. "But first, what were you saying to your mother about 'just like Father'?"

"The same thing he has been saying ever since he started watching you and Red Cloud training his uncle," Gentle Fawn said. "Quiet Thunder wants to be a great warrior like his father."

Fire Eagle smiled and lifted the boy to his shoulders. "If Quiet Thunder is to be a great warrior, he must learn to ride a horse!" Fire Eagle stepped outside and began to gallop around, rearing and neighing. Others looked on, smiling indulgently.

Wagon trains were coming west by the dozens from their jumping off places in St. Joseph and Independence, Missouri. With the influx of the trains, more buffalo were being shot and left to rot, and the Indians were growing more hostile.

During the first week of September, Gray Shadow met with chiefs of the Hunkpapa, Brule, and Miniconjou Sioux tribes, and several Cheyenne, Arapaho, and Blackfeet chiefs. It was agreed that the wagon trains would be attacked without letup. The whites needed to learn they were not welcome in Indian territory.

In the next few days, soldiers from every fort were pressed into action. Word spread quickly of the bloodshed on the wagon trails, and the powers in Washington reacted by sending more soldiers and hastening the construction of more forts.

The chiefs unleashed their warriors on the construction crews, attacking them fiercely and setting their partially constructed stockades on fire. And the army fought back.

It was October 3, 1858, when young Curly killed his first soldier in battle and won his right to wear a feather in his headband. He was now a Sioux warrior. From then on he fought battle after battle alongside Fire Eagle and Red Cloud.

As winter set in, the fighting dwindled to periodic skirmishes. But when spring came, the wagon trains arrived in droves and once again felt the wrath of the Plains Indians...and the Indians the wrath of the army.

Fire Eagle had devised a plan, which the Sioux and their allies put into effect. Since the army wagon trains were driving beef cattle from the stockyards in Kansas City and other places to supply meat for the forts, the Indians would concentrate on stampeding the cattle. While part of them attacked the soldiers in the trains, the rest of them would follow the cattle, shoot them down, and use them for meat and other products.

Gray Shadow was well pleased with the success of Fire Eagle's plan.

In May 1859, an army wagon train heading to Fort Laramie was driving two hundred head of cattle. The soldiers were elated as they neared the Nebraska-Wyoming border. They had come all the way across Nebraska Territory without incident.

They entered a long, shallow valley. Before they got halfway across, three hundred warriors, their faces bright with war paint, came swooping over the north ridge.

There were 111 officers and troopers in the train. The cattle stampeded almost immediately as the Indians came at a full gallop, some firing muskets, others shooting arrows.

Young Curly, eager to make good, killed three soldiers. His courage and fierceness in battle was not overlooked by his father, nor by Fire Eagle or Red Cloud, who was now a sub-chief and showing magnificent leadership ability.

Two days later, a scout patrol went out from Fort Laramie, looking for the overdue wagon train and cattle. When they dropped into the valley, they were sickened at what lay before them. All the soldiers had been killed, as well as their horses and mules. The cattle were gone. A few pintos lay dead, but the bodies of their riders had been carried away.

It was evident that after the ammunition was spent, there had been a savage hand-to-hand battle. The Indians had swarmed the soldiers, overwhelming them. It was common practice for Sioux and Cheyenne to take the scalps and mutilate the bodies of their dead enemies. This battle had been no exception.

Washington went into action, trying to offset the devastation of military manpower and loss of cattle. The federal government was going to have to provide more soldiers and better weapons if they wanted to win the West. Washington responded as best it could. Pressure was put on weapons manufacturers to design and produce faster-loading firearms, and army camps were training men as fast as they could.

In July 1860, Gray Shadow made a difficult decision. He had lost a great many warriors in the battles with the army and was unable to replace them. He made a trip to an Oglala village in southern Dakota Territory, under the rule of Chief Big Thumb, who was old and in poor health. Big Thumb agreed to step down as chief if Gray Shadow would bring his Oglala tribe to the village. Gray Shadow would become chief of the combined population.

Upon returning to the village in Nebraska Territory, Gray Shadow told his people of the agreement, and they packed up and headed north. Hungry Bear would humbly serve under Gray Shadow, knowing he would no doubt remain a sub-chief for the rest of his life. There was no question that Fire Eagle would become chief in his father's stead when Gray Shadow had to step down because of age or ill health.

As they made the long, tedious trek north, Gentle Fawn thought of her dear friend, Andrea Tyler. Fire Eagle had told Gentle Fawn that the new Oglala village was located on a choice piece of land near the spot where the White Clay River and the Bad River joined—about twenty-five miles southwest of Fort Pierre. If the Tylers were still at Fort Pierre, Gentle Fawn would find a way to see Andrea.

When they arrived at the two rivers, the men went to work setting up the teepees. Gray Shadow and Fire Eagle were immediately called to what would be a lengthy powwow with elderly Chief Big Thumb.

As Red Cloud and Curly were setting up Gentle Fawn's teepee—with seven-year-old Quiet Thunder's help—Curly noticed her looking toward the northeast.

"Is the sister of this warrior thinking of Andrea Tyler?"

"Yes, my brother. It has been so long since I have seen her."

"She may not be there any longer," Red Cloud said. "The army moves its officers from fort to fort."

Gentle Fawn looked at her brother. "If Curly loves his sister," she said, "he will ride to the trading post outside Fort Pierre and ask the soldier coats if Lieutenant Colonel Tyler and his family are still there."

As Gentle Fawn's words hung in the air, Curly glanced at Red Cloud, then said, "Curly does love his sister. But he is not eager to mingle with white eyes."

"If Father will allow me, I will go for you, Mother," Quiet Thunder said.

Curly looked at his nephew and sighed. "You make me feel ashamed, Quiet Thunder." Then to his sister, "I will go, Gentle Fawn. As soon as we have finished setting up the teepee."

"Mother, may I go with him?"

"Only if your father gives permission."

Curly knew he could break in on a powwow if the matter was important, and any wish of Quiet Thunder's was an important matter in the eyes of Fire Eagle.

An hour later, Curly stepped inside the teepee and said, "I have good news, my nephew. Your father says you can go with me to the trading post. He says with you along, there will be less chance of a problem arising with white eyes."

Uncle and nephew galloped out of the village riding double. Nearly two hours later, they arrived at the trading post, which stood just outside the stockade walls of Fort Pierre. There was little activity; three soldiers stood outside talking to a couple of unkempt buffalo hunters. There were two pintos standing nearby, whisking flies off, and a single wagon parked beside them.

When uncle and nephew entered the building, they saw a white man and his wife at the counter and two middle-aged Blackfeet browsing along one wall.

Quiet Thunder was fascinated by all the different items that lined the shelves, but he knew better than to handle any of them. While he gazed at the shelves, Curly watched for an opportunity to ask about the Tylers. When two of the soldiers from outside stepped in, Curly approached them. "I am Curly of the Oglala Sioux. May I ask you a question?"

The soldier nodded with little expression on his face.

"I am wondering if Lieutenant Colonel Theron Tyler and his family are still at Fort Pierre."

"You know the Tylers, do you?"

"Yes," Curly said, laying a hand on top of Quiet Thunder's head. "My nephew here was born on the same day as Colonel Tyler's son, Thann. Both were born at our village, which was near Point Nemaha in Nebraska Territory."

"The colonel's son was born in an Indian village?"

"That is correct."

"Hmm. That's interesting. Well, yes, they're still here."

"Thank you," Curly said, forcing a smile.

As he and Quiet Thunder stepped outside, they noticed that the buffalo hunters were gone. The third soldier was standing alone, watching the approach of four riders. Curly knew by the pelts on the pack mule that they were trappers. They were all heavily bearded and almost as dirty-looking as the buffalo hunters.

As the trappers dismounted, Curly's eyes settled on the features of one and stayed there. Something about the face...

Suddenly the twenty-year-old Sioux warrior went back in his mind seven years. The mouth. Yes, the turned-down mouth! No, it could not be. The beard made it difficult to be sure.

"Hey Dolan," one of the trappers said, "let's start the price high. If he don't take it, we can always come down a bit."

"Sure, why not?" Dolan said.

It *was* him! William Dolan—the army lieutenant who had murdered the old people in the village and shot down Curly's mother. An old hatred boiled up within him like the fire and brimstone of a live volcano.

C H A P T E R
FOURTEEN

Quiet Thunder saw his uncle stiffen and his mouth curl into a wolfish snarl. He started to ask what was wrong, but Curly silenced him with a hand signal.

Each trapper carried an armload of pelts inside the trading post and the lone soldier followed them through the door. Curly looked around; there was no one else in sight.

"Curly, do you know those men?" Quiet Thunder asked.

"I know one of them." Curly headed toward Dolan's horse and slipped the musket from Dolan's saddleboot. "Come on," he said, hurrying to the side of the building while checking to see if the gun was loaded.

Curly slipped up to one of the side windows and carefully peered in. Quiet Thunder waited patiently, eyeing the musket in his uncle's hands.

Curly watched as Dolan and the other trappers discussed prices with the proprietor. Soon a deal was struck, the pelts were piled on the counter, and everyone turned jovial.

After a few moments, Dolan told the others he needed to go to the privy out back. He would return in a few minutes.

Curly glanced at the open area in front of the trading post. Still no one had shown up. "Quiet Thunder, go get the pinto. Bring him to the side of the building. Wait right back here at the rear corner, but keep out of sight from the privy."

"What is the privy?"

"It is a very small building out in the back. Do as I tell you, and wait for me."

While Quiet Thunder did as his uncle said, Curly eased to the corner of the building. He heard the back door open and slam shut, then peered around the corner. The man he had hated for a third of his life was walking to the small structure with the steep roof and the half-moon cut in its door.

Curly looked around again to make sure no one was watching. He cocked the hammer of the musket and hastened across the open area, halting some ten feet from the privy door.

His heart pounded in his breast. Finally, the day of reckoning had come. He would shoot Dolan only if he was forced to do so. His plan was to kill the man as he had always dreamed—with his bare hands.

When the ex-lieutenant stepped out, he found himself looking down the menacing bore of his own musket. He raised his palms. "Hey, hey, hey there, young fella! What's this all about?"

"It is about what you did seven years ago. You killed helpless old people, and you shot my mother."

Dolan wanted to call for help, but he knew it would put a bullet in his heart. Tears filled his eyes as he kept his hands at shoulder level and said with quivering lips, "What do you want?"

"I want you dead, *Lieutenant* Dolan…like you made those poor old people of my village, and like you meant to make my mother."

Dolan remembered the Indian woman who had thrown the rock and hit him in the head. One of his men had shot her. He remembered seeing her at Fort Clark. Suddenly it all came back. This was the boy who had jumped on his back and almost clawed his eyes out.

"You…you ain't gonna shoot me down right here!"

Curly's finger raised slightly from the trigger, then eased

down again, but he did not reply.

"You pull that trigger, you'll have those soldiers in there on top of you," Dolan said.

"Unbuckle your gunbelt."

"Why?"

"Do as I tell you!" Curly waved the muzzle threateningly.

Dolan lowered his hands slowly while keeping his gaze on the warrior's eyes. He let his gunbelt drop to the ground.

"Kick it over here to me. Now, I will give you a chance to live, *Lieutenant.* That is more than you gave the people in my village."

Dolan frowned. "What do you mean?"

"We will fight with no weapons."

"You mean barehanded? You and me?"

"Yes. We will fight barehanded to the death. Is it agreed?"

Dolan could hardly believe his ears. This young warrior was muscular, but he outweighed him an easy seventy pounds. Besides, Dolan had learned that a man should always have a back-up plan. His was strapped to the back of his pants belt. The knife only had a four-inch blade, but in Bill Dolan's hand, it had proven lethal on more than a few occasions.

Dolan's hands dangled at his sides. He raised an arm and sleeved the tears from his eyes. "I agree to that," he said. "A fight to the death...no weapons."

Quiet Thunder peered around the corner of the building and looked the husky trapper up and down. The man was much heavier than his uncle. He blinked when he saw Curly ease down the hammer of the musket and lay it on the ground.

Curly was still bent over when Dolan reached behind his back and charged forward like a bull. Curly rushed to meet him, his hands splayed and ready for action. Suddenly he saw the flash of metal.

Curly seized the upraised arm as Dolan's beefy body struck him full-on. He went down with Dolan on top, yet he clung tenaciously to the thick wrist, holding the short-bladed knife away.

Curly heaved upward and yanked Dolan's arm sideways with surprising force, rolling him on his side. Curly unleashed a jarring blow that stunned Dolan momentarily, and Curly was able to wrest the knife from his grasp. Eyes bulging with fury, Curly hissed, "You have lying tongue, white man! You agree to fight with no weapon, then pull the knife! I give the knife back to you!"

Dolan tried to grab Curly's wrist, but the knife flashed down and pierced his heart.

Curly looked down at the dead man, feeling the sweetness of revenge, then dashed toward Quiet Thunder and the pinto.

Fire Eagle was watching Red Cloud work with several young would-be warriors, when he saw Curly and Quiet Thunder trot into the village.

He excused himself and headed for his teepee, where Gentle Fawn and her parents were talking outside. Fire Eagle walked up as Curly said, "They are still there, my sister."

"I am so glad," she said. "I must find a way to visit Andrea." She cocked her head to one side. "You look very happy, Curly. Did you see the Tylers, perhaps?"

"No. A soldier coat at the trading post told me they are still there."

Fire Eagle could read the joy in his brother-in-law's eyes. "Tell us what happened to make you so happy," he said.

Curly turned to his mother. "You carry a scar on your body because a soldier coat shot you."

White Wing's brow furrowed.

"You threw a rock and hit the lieutenant named Dolan who was killing our people."

"I did," White Wing replied, "and one of his men shot me."

"You remember that I almost clawed Dolan's eyes out at Fort Clark."

"How could we forget?" Gentle Fawn said. "Are you about to tell us that you have seen this Lieutenant Dolan?"

Curly's smile broadened. "I did. At the trading post."

"And he killed him, too!" Quiet Thunder said.

Curly nodded, a victorious smile on his lips. "I had given up ever laying eyes on Dolan, but there he was, along with some other men who trap small animals and sell their skins to white traders. They came to sell skins to the man who owns the trading post. I followed Dolan when he went out behind the trading post."

"Curly killed the bad man with his own knife," Quiet Thunder said.

Laughing Horse spoke up. "Did the other white men see you do this?"

"No, Father," Curly said. "Dolan and I fought with only Quiet Thunder watching. I have long dreamed of killing that devil man with my bare hands. He agreed to fight me to the death with no weapons, but when he came at me, he pulled a knife. I used it to kill him."

Laughing Horse nodded and said no more.

Quiet Thunder turned to Gentle Fawn. "Mother, I would like to know more about this Lieutenant Dolan and what he did at our village on the day I was born. I asked Curly to tell me while we were riding back here. He said you and Father should tell me."

Fire Eagle laid a hand on Quiet Thunder's shoulder. "Gentle Fawn, I think our son is ready to listen. Since I was not there on that day, it is best that you tell the story."

"All right," she said. "Let us sit down."

Gentle Fawn gave her son every detail of that day, including John Stranger's part.

"Why have you not told me this before, Mother?"

"Because we wanted you to be old enough to grasp it, Son," Fire Eagle answered for his squaw.

"I would like to meet this man who saved our lives. Where does John Stranger live?"

"We do not know," Gentle Fawn said. "We have not seen him since that day. I will be back in a moment." She dashed inside the teepee and returned quickly. Sitting down face-to-face with her son, she opened her palm and let him see the shiny silver disk.

"What is it, Mother?"

"It is what white men call a medallion. Remember I told you a little while ago that John Stranger disappeared quite suddenly that day?"

"Yes."

"He left this behind. It was next to your crib."

"May I see it?" Quiet Thunder examined the disk carefully. "What are these words?"

"They are from the white man's Book, called the Bible. You have seen the black Book I keep in the box. You asked me about it when you were younger. I told you it was left to me by the missionary Paul Breland."

"Yes."

"The words say that John Stranger is from a far land."

"What far land, Mother?"

"It does not say. We just know that the Sky Father sent John Stranger to us that day to save our lives."

"Will he ever come back?"

"There is no way to know. Probably not."

"May I have the medallion, Mother?"

Gentle Fawn looked at her husband, then said, "Your father and I discussed it some time ago. We planned to give it to you, but not until you are sixteen grasses and make your first wild animal kill. We will give it to you then, and you can wear it on the leather thong around your neck with the wild animal's paw."

Quiet Thunder nodded. "That will be good," he said, handing the medallion back to her. "I will look forward to the day I can wear it."

"There was something else that happened on the day you

were born, Quiet Thunder," Gentle Fawn said. "I have waited to tell you about it also, because I wanted it to mean something to you."

"Yes, Mother?"

"You have heard me talk much of Andrea Tyler."

"Yes. And her husband, the soldier coat. And their son who is my age—Thann. We used to play together. I do not remember him, but that is what you have told me."

"That's right. Only I have not told you that Thann and you were born on the same day. Thann Tyler was born in our teepee."

Quiet Thunder's eyes widened. "A white boy born in an Indian teepee? How did this happen?"

Gentle Fawn told him about the army wagon train swinging into the village on its way to Fort Clark because Major Tyler had sensed something was wrong.

"Mother, I would like to see Thann Tyler. Even though he is a white boy, we should become friends since he was born in our teepee."

"Now that we know the Tylers are still at Fort Pierre, we will find a way to see them," she said.

Curly had lived in his own teepee since becoming a warrior. That evening, as darkness fell, he decided to go into the woods alone to commune with the Sky Father and thank him for delivering the evil Lieutenant Dolan into his hands.

Moonlight made a dappled carpet on the grass beneath the tall cottonwoods as Curly slid off his pinto and sat down, leaning his back against a tree. There he prayed to the Sky Father.

Soon he felt drowsy. He stretched out on the grass and instantly fell asleep and began to dream. In the dream, he saw a yellow-spotted war horse floating as in a mist. The horse was dancing about in circles, neighing with elation, acting as if it had gone crazy with joy. Curly understood why the horse was acting in this manner. It was expressing the happiness Curly felt in his heart to have killed Lieutenant Dolan.

When Curly awakened, he felt refreshed and rode back to his teepee.

The next morning, Curly told his parents what had happened in the woods the night before. As a medicine man, Laughing Horse was especially interested in Curly's dream. He asked his son to tell him the dream again, making sure he left nothing out. The medicine man closed his eyes, touching his temples in deep concentration. When Curly had finished telling it the second time, Laughing Horse opened his eyes. "Wakan Tanka has made me to understand."

"The dream has significance, Father?"

"Yes. The dancing war horse in your dream was you, my son. You are to become among the mightiest of Lakota warriors and will be a great leader of warriors. Wakan Tanka wishes you to take on a new name. Your name is now Crazy Horse."

Curly's faith in his father was unfaltering. "It is as you say, my father. My name is now Crazy Horse."

When Laughing Horse told Gray Shadow the dream, Gray Shadow gave orders for the tribe to come together. Laughing Horse stood before them all, announcing that Wakan Tanka had given Curly a new name, for he was destined to become a great leader of warriors.

Early the next morning, Gray Shadow and Fire Eagle rode out of the village with a dozen warriors, including Red Cloud, for a two-day ride west. A powwow had been called by Hunkpapa Sioux Chief Sitting Bull at his village. Cheyenne, Arapaho, and Blackfeet chiefs and sub-chiefs would be there. Sitting Bull, who was rising to fame among the Plains Indians as a brilliant battle strategist, wanted to organize the tribes to fight the growing numbers of whites swarming into Indian territory.

Crazy Horse had stayed behind to help his sister contact

Andrea Tyler before things heated up once again between Indians and whites. They planned to take Quiet Thunder and ride to Fort Pierre, under a white flag, and ask to see Lieutenant Colonel Tyler. If he was not at the fort, Gentle Fawn would ask the soldier coats to bring Andrea Tyler to the gate.

"We will go now," Crazy Horse said. "I will bridle our horses. Quiet Thunder can ride with me."

As Crazy Horse headed toward the rope corral, his attention was drawn to two warriors running toward him. Beyond them were more warriors, along with women and children, staring off to the northeast.

"Crazy Horse! An army wagon is coming! There are riders, too. One of them is carrying a white flag!"

Crazy Horse could now see a woman in a sunbonnet and a small boy beside the driver. A soldier coat rode beside them

He turned to look for his sister and saw that she was already coming toward him with Quiet Thunder by her side.

"I think it is Andrea Tyler on the wagon seat," Crazy Horse said.

Gentle Fawn's heart beat faster as she hurried to the front of the crowd with Quiet Thunder at her side.

Many of the people were not part of Gray Shadow's village from Point Nemaha, and they knew nothing of the relationship between the Tylers and Fire Eagle's family. Crazy Horse calmed them, saying there were few white eyes he did not hate. The Tylers were those few. They could be trusted. As long as Lieutenant Colonel Tyler was present, the other soldier coats would cause no trouble.

The instant the procession halted, Andrea was out of the wagon without help from her husband. The dark-haired boy with sky-blue eyes was right behind her.

As Andrea and Gentle Fawn ran to each other, Tyler dismounted and told the great crowd of Oglalas that they had come in peace. The warriors looked at Tyler and the other men in blue coats with skepticism, then led their families back to the village. Soon only the Tylers and Fire Eagle's family were left.

Thann and Quiet Thunder stood several feet apart, studying each other, while Gentle Fawn explained that Fire Eagle was on a journey with Gray Shadow. She told them of Curly's name change, then took Quiet Thunder by the hand and led him to Thann. Andrea and Theron looked on, smiling.

"Hello, Thann," Gentle Fawn said. "I do not suppose you remember me?"

"No, ma'am. I know who you are because Mommy talks about you a lot, but I guess I was too little the last time I saw you."

"Andrea, does Thann know where he was born, and that he and Quiet Thunder were born on the same day?"

"Oh, yes. He knows the whole story."

She turned back to Thann and smiled. "It has been my dream, Thann, that you and Quiet Thunder could meet again."

"Son," Andrea said, "Daddy taught you to shake hands Indian-style. How about you boys shaking hands?"

Quiet Thunder and Thann gripped forearms, then Quiet Thunder said, "Would you like to see my frogs? I have five of them at the river in a box my father made me."

Thann's eyes lit up. "I sure would!"

While the boys played together on the river bank, a strong bond formed between them. Just before they were summoned to the village so the Tylers could head back to Fort Pierre, Thann and Quiet Thunder agreed that even though whites and Indians were enemies, they would always be friends.

FIFTEEN

O ver the next several months, the Sioux nation and their Cheyenne, Arapaho, and Blackfeet allies discussed how they would fight the whites who kept crossing their land and even settling on it.

During that same time of relative peace, Andrea Tyler and Gentle Fawn spent a good deal of time together, which allowed their sons to deepen their friendship. The boys became so close they secretly shared the wish that they could be brothers.

The Civil War broke out in April 1861, and Theron Tyler was sent east to fight on the Union side. Andrea and her son stayed at Fort Pierre, since it was now their home.

There was little fighting between whites and Indians while the Civil War raged, though there were some tribes in Texas, New Mexico, and Colorado who joined the Union or Confederate side to fight.

In March 1863, Gray Shadow took ill with pneumonia and died, leaving Fire Eagle as chief of the tribe.

On Thann and Quiet Thunder's tenth birthday, the Tylers gave each boy a new Winchester .44 carbine. The boys had already been trained with shoulder arms by their fathers and were good shots.

They were eager to try their skills with the new guns and

went into the forest a few miles northwest of the village, accompanied by Fire Eagle. When the hunt was over, each boy had bagged a large buck deer. Fire Eagle boasted to Andrea that they were natural-born warriors.

In early September 1863, Chief Fire Eagle and a small band of Oglalas were returning from a Blackfoot village some thirty miles due north of their village. Fire Eagle wore his full headdress. Red Cloud, the highest ranking sub-chief, rode on Fire Eagle's right. Crazy Horse, who was also a sub-chief, rode on his left. In respect for their chief, both men let Fire Eagle ride a half-length ahead of them.

They had just held a powwow with the Blackfeet, linking the two tribes into a stronger alliance. Fire Eagle was pleased with the results.

It was midafternoon as the Oglalas passed through a shallow valley between two ridges.

Fort Bennett was fifty miles west of Fort Pierre, on the Cheyenne River. The north-south dividing line for patrols between the two forts was Digger's Creek, five miles east of the valley where the Oglalas were now riding.

Lieutenant Craig Skehan and nine troopers from Fort Bennett were finished with their routine patrol and were returning to the fort. As they reached the east crest of the valley, Sergeant Clayton Hansford's eye caught movement.

"Look, Lieutenant! Indians down there!"

"Get back, before they see us!" Skehan said.

The troopers turned their mounts and moved below the ridge line.

Skehan dismounted, slipped a pair of binoculars out of his

saddlebags, and crawled to the crest of the ridge. Hansford dropped down beside him.

"My guess is around a dozen of them, sir," Hansford said. "How close am I?"

"Fourteen."

"Four more than us. Maybe we can take 'em, since we have the element of surprise."

"I'm not interested in getting into a battle with them," Skehan said, still peering through binoculars. "I just want to drop one of them off his horse."

"Excuse me, sir?"

"There's a chief leading them. Full headdress. He's Sioux, but I don't know who he is. Depends on what village he's from. No way to know whether they're coming or going from their home village. I sure would like to get a chief, though. Tell Benson to bring me his rifle."

Trooper Benson carried a Sharps .44 caliber rifle with an extra long barrel for accuracy. It was equipped with a new telescopic sight.

Trooper Benson crawled up the ridge and handed Skehan the rifle. "It's ready to fire, sir," he said.

"When I knock that dirty redskin off his horse," Skehan said, "you men be ready to ride. I'll come on the run the instant I see him go down."

The two soldiers hurried back to the others and quickly mounted up. Hansford leaned from his saddle and held the reins of Skehan's horse at the bit.

The Oglalas in the valley were discussing how they would hold a similar meeting with Cheyenne and Arapaho chiefs. Better coordination among the allies would create stronger defenses against the white-eyes army and its increasingly superior fire power.

"Fire Eagle," Crazy Horse said, "it is my thought that if we come to all-out war with the whites, we should work closer with Chief Sitting Bull. He has proven himself very clever when it comes to planning battles."

"I agree," Fire Eagle said, the breeze toying with his colorful headdress. "Chief Sitting Bull's tactics are far superior to—"

A bullet tore into Fire Eagle's chest, followed by the sharp crack of a rifle echoing across the valley.

Red Cloud glimpsed a blue-white puff of smoke on the distant ridge before he reached out to Fire Eagle. But Crazy Horse already had a firm grip on him.

Red Cloud quickly slid off his horse and took Fire Eagle in his arms. He looked back to the spot where he'd seen the puff of smoke. "It had to be soldier coats. Our Indian enemies have no rifle that will shoot so far."

Red Cloud knelt to lay Fire Eagle on the ground. He checked for pulse and breath and then looked up at his companions. "Chief Fire Eagle is dead."

Crazy Horse beat his chest and lifted his rifle defiantly. "Dirty devil soldier coats! I hate soldier coats! I kill all soldier coats!" He goaded his horse and galloped full-speed toward the east ridge.

"He will never catch the rifleman," Red Cloud said. "Let us take our beloved chief home."

The western sky was vivid with sunset's colors as the Oglala band rode into the village with Fire Eagle's body. Word reached Gentle Fawn and Quiet Thunder in their teepee, and they came running up as Red Cloud was handing the limp form to two warriors.

Gentle Fawn reached out to touch her husband. "No! No-o-o! Wakan Tanka, do not let it be! No-o!" White Wing pushed her way through the crowd and took Gentle Fawn in her arms.

Quiet Thunder had seen many a dead warrior carried into the Oglala village, but this was his father. He felt his grandfather lift him to his chest and hold him close.

Red Cloud explained to Gentle Fawn and all the Oglalas what had happened in the valley. When White Wing asked where Crazy Horse was, Red Cloud told her he had ridden off after the murderer.

"He will only get himself killed," Laughing Horse said. "No doubt there were many soldier coats on the ridge."

Fire Eagle's body was placed on a death scaffold. When the wailing of the people had died out and the fires were doused, the sad villagers scattered to their teepees.

Late in the night, Quiet Thunder awakened to find his mother asleep with the black Book in her hand and a candle still burning.

He reached out to gently slip the Bible from her fingers, but she woke up. "Son, why are you awake at this time of night?"

"The pain in my heart must have awakened me. Why were you reading the white man's Bible, Mother? White men are bad. All of them except Thann and his parents are bad."

"Missionary Paul Breland was not bad, Son," she said, stroking his hair. "He loved us. And John Stranger was not bad. He saved our lives and the life of your grandmother."

Quiet Thunder thought of the silver medallion and the man who had left it behind. "But other than those, there never have been any good white people. I cannot wait to grow up so I can kill the soldier coats. I hate white eyes!"

Gentle Fawn was too weary to lecture her son on hatred and killing, and at the moment she did not want to answer his question as to why she had been reading the Bible. "Go back to sleep, Quiet Thunder," she said.

"Mother, when will Uncle Curly—I mean, Uncle Crazy Horse—come home?"

"I do not know." She sighed and blew out the candle. "You go to sleep."

Gentle Fawn rolled over and went to sleep. When she awoke

it was still dark outside, but there was enough starlight coming through the teepee opening to show her that Quiet Thunder was not on his pallet.

She rose and stepped outside into the night air, which was cool and refreshing. All was still. She could hear snores coming from the surrounding teepees. Gentle Fawn hurried to the edge of the village where the lone death scaffold stood tall against the star-lit sky. Quiet Thunder was sitting on the ground, leaning against one of its poles and sobbing.

Quiet Thunder raised his head and looked at his mother through tear-dimmed eyes. He drew a shuddering breath. "I want my father to be alive! Wakan Tanka can make him live. I know he can."

Gentle Fawn pulled her son close and said, "Wakan Tanka does not make people alive after Ynke-lo takes them, my son. We must keep your father alive in our hearts by holding our memories of him there. Come, now. You must return to your bed."

Word soon traveled to Fort Pierre of Chief Fire Eagle's death. The day after Red Cloud officially became chief, an army wagon with an escort carrying a white flag arrived at the Oglala village. Andrea Tyler—whose husband was still fighting in the Civil War—and son Thann had come to express their grief and to give what comfort they could to Gentle Fawn and Quiet Thunder.

Thann's presence at the time of Quiet Thunder's deepest grief endeared him even more to his best friend.

On the eighth day after Fire Eagle's death, the body was lowered into the ground with the entire village in attendance. There were also several chiefs from Cheyenne, Arapaho, and Blackfeet tribes there.

Laughing Horse stood at the grave, chanting in a high-pitched wail as the body was covered with dirt. From where Gentle Fawn stood with Quiet Thunder, she saw her brother return to camp and move toward them through the crowd with a dark object in his hand.

Crazy Horse slipped up beside Gentle Fawn and White Wing and stood in silence through the rest of the ceremony. When it was over and the crowd was breaking up, Gentle Fawn turned to her brother. "You have been gone a long time, Crazy Horse."

He had the same kind of light in his eye as the day he had killed Bill Dolan.

"I have been gone many days because it took me that long to find the skunk-bear soldier coat who shot Fire Eagle."

"You found him, Uncle?" Quiet Thunder asked.

"The tracks on top of east ridge led to Fort Bennett. Crazy Horse wait until he can capture one soldier coat outside of fort alone. A yellow-bellied soldier coat will tell much when he is hurting bad. He seemed glad to tell me who it was who shot Fire Eagle and to give me his description."

Crazy Horse lifted the object in his hand and revealed a forelock of thick black hair.

In the spring of 1864, the Crow and Shoshone Indians were giving Sitting Bull's Hunkpapa Sioux and many other Sioux tribes serious trouble. Sitting Bull had sent messengers, asking Red Cloud to move his village nearer the Wyoming border. Once more Andrea and Gentle Fawn said goodbye without knowing if they would ever see each other again.

Red Cloud settled his village on a small creek just four miles east of Sitting Bull's village. Both needed the space to satisfy their independence.

As time passed, Quiet Thunder worked at his skills with rifle, knife, spear, and tomahawk. The big dream to become a warrior was still alive in his heart, especially as he watched Chief Red Cloud and his Oglala warriors join with Sitting Bull's Hunkpapa warriors and other Sioux tribes to fight the Crows and the Shoshones.

In April 1865, the Civil War came to a close, and brevet Brigadier General Theron Tyler returned to Fort Pierre in late May. On the day after he arrived at the fort, Tyler knocked on Colonel Cady's door.

"You wanted to see me, sir?"

"Yes. Sit down."

"I guess this is the moment I drop back to lieutenant colonel, right, sir? "

"Yes, the brevet period is over," Cady said, "and I'm glad it is. This country has been at war too long."

"Can't disagree with that, sir."

"However, my friend, I have a telegram from Washington that you are to be made a full colonel just before you become commandant at Fort Laramie."

"Fort Laramie, sir?"

"As you know, there's a lot of Indian trouble festering in western Nebraska and Wyoming. The wire I received said the commandant is retiring from military service. Your promotion should come through in about five or six weeks."

Andrea was very happy with her husband's promotion, but his becoming commandant at Fort Laramie was a bit unnerving. The news of accelerating Indian trouble had come from that direction for several weeks.

"You know I have no choice in the matter, sweetheart. If you would rather move back East with some of your relatives, I would understand."

"Oh, no you don't!" She threw her arms around his neck. "We've been apart for four years. No more of that. Thann and I are going with you to Fort Laramie."

"I hoped you'd say that. I sure don't want to be away from you anymore."

"Theron, do you know why the Indians are stirring up more trouble further west?"

"The government's taking their land, and they're planning to take even more. Not only that, but the Indians are resisting the westward move of thousands of white people since the War ended."

The Tylers arrived with an escort at Fort Laramie on July 24, 1865. Colonel Frank Hammond turned his command over to Tyler immediately, and he and his wife headed east with the escort returning to Fort Pierre.

Twelve-year-old Thann Tyler dreamed of the day he would attend West Point as his forebears had. The military had been in his blood from the moment he was born.

On a hot day in 1867, Quiet Thunder was hunting squirrels in the woods three or four miles from the Oglala village when he heard sudden, rapid gunfire. He turned and saw several Crow Indians riding across an open field, heading for the forest where he stood. Crazy Horse and a band of Oglalas were on their heels, firing as they rode.

Quiet Thunder's heart pounded as he dashed to a thicket of bushes and ducked down. He loaded his nine-shot Winchester

.44 carbine and peered through the bushes. Soon he saw two Crow come within thirty yards of where he crouched. Both Indians chose a tree and started to climb.

Quiet Thunder worked the lever of his carbine and jacked a cartridge into the chamber. Quickly shouldering the rifle, he took aim at the Crow who had climbed the highest and squeezed the trigger. The bullet met its mark.

The other Crow paused on a lower limb and brought his musket up. Before he could fire, Quiet Thunder fired again. The Crow was dead before he hit the ground.

Suddenly there was a rustle of grass and brush. Quiet Thunder turned to see his uncle and another Oglala warrior named Wind Hawk on foot, carrying their rifles.

Crazy Horse stiffened when he recognized his nephew and saw him standing over the two dead Crow. "Quiet Thunder! What are you doing here?"

"Hunting squirrels."

"Did *you* kill these two?"

"Yes. They were climbing the trees so they could shoot our warriors."

Crazy Horse shook his head in disbelief. "Quiet Thunder, that is a brave thing you did, but you must go home. Where is your pinto?"

"In the brush back there."

"Get on it immediately and go home."

Without another word, Crazy Horse ran toward the battle with Wind Hawk on his heels.

Quiet Thunder's heart pumped with exhilaration as he ran after them. He had not gone far when he saw Crazy Horse and Wind Hawk pull up behind trees and begin firing at enemy warriors Quiet Thunder could not see.

He took shelter behind a cottonwood some forty feet from them. Movement caught his eye to the left. A Crow warrior was drawing a bead on Wind Hawk.

Quiet Thunder took quick aim and fired. The Crow let out a shrill cry and fell. Both Crazy Horse and Wind Hawk stopped firing and looked around. They saw the Crow warrior on the ground and smoke lifting from Quiet Thunder's gun muzzle.

"He was aiming at Wind Hawk!" Quiet Thunder said.

A short time later, the Crow were on the run. The Oglalas let them go and gathered to count their losses. In front of all the warriors, Wind Hawk praised Quiet Thunder for saving his life. When the warriors asked what the boy was doing fighting in the battle, Crazy Horse said that Quiet Thunder was hunting squirrels when the fight came into the forest.

Wind Hawk and Crazy Horse reported Quiet Thunder's kills to Chief Red Cloud, and Quiet Thunder was publicly rewarded and commended for his bravery and skill. But he was told he was still too young to go into battle.

SIXTEEN

In early June 1868, Quiet Thunder was hunting alone, hoping to kill a deer to take home to his mother. After more than an hour of stealthy movement through the dense trees, Quiet Thunder saw a large buck with a huge set of antlers, nibbling from a low-hanging elm branch. Such antlers would give bragging rights in the Oglala village.

Quiet Thunder moved behind a large cottonwood and shouldered his rifle. He drew a bead, took a breath and held it. Suddenly the buck jerked its head in the opposite direction and bolted into the deep shade of the forest before Quiet Thunder could get off a shot.

He heard three rifle shots in rapid succession and then some youthful male voices complaining jovially about missing the buck. He caught a glimpse through the trees and squinted to bring one boy's face into clearer focus. It was his best friend! Quiet Thunder had not seen Thann since they'd said goodbye four years earlier.

As the boys headed away from him, Quiet Thunder cupped a hand to his mouth and shouted, "Thann! Thann Tyler!"

Thann said something to his companions and ran back. "Quiet Thunder! My friend!"

The other two boys looked on with gaping mouths as

Thann and Quiet Thunder embraced, pounding each other on the back.

Thann kept an arm around Quiet Thunder's shoulder and guided him toward his companions. "I want you to meet the best friend I have in all the world! Tommy Patterson...Neil Frame, meet Quiet Thunder. Tommy and Neil are officers' sons at Fort Laramie," Thann said, smiling. "Just like me."

"You are at Fort Laramie? I did not know that. I am sure my mother does not know it either."

"Pa's the commandant," Thann said. "We came here almost three years ago."

Neil moved close and said, "Thann, how come this Indian is your best friend? Don't you know Indians are cold-blooded killers and they torture white people?"

"Yeah," Tommy said. "They're our enemies. How come you'd be friends with a scummy redskin?"

Thann fought to push anger away as he said, "Maybe some Indians are scummy, Patterson. Just like some white people are scummy. But Quiet Thunder's people took care of my mother and me when I was born. Ma says they treated us real good. And as for you, Neil, there are plenty of white people who kill Indians, and I happen to know of some who've tortured Indians, too. Quiet Thunder and his mother are not our enemies. His mom and my mom are best friends, too."

"Then you and your mom are traitors, Thann!" Neil said. "Indians are our enemies, so if you make friends with 'em, you're a traitor!"

Thann's anger got the best of him. "You two don't know what you're talking about! Quiet Thunder and his mom are not our enemies!"

"C'mon, Tommy," Neil said. "Let's go do our huntin' some-where else. I don't wanna be around this Indian lover."

"Go ahead!" Thann said. "I don't want to be around you, either!"

When the pair had passed from view, Quiet Thunder said, "I am sorry to cause you trouble with your friends."

"Don't give it another thought, Quiet Thunder. They're not real friends if they act like that."

"I am glad your father made it through the War, Thann. Was he wounded?"

"Yes, but it wasn't anything real bad. Just some shrapnel."

As Quiet Thunder and Thann stood talking, two Shoshones crept up behind some nearby trees.

"How is your mother?" Thann asked.

"She is fine. She— "

Quiet Thunder moved with the swiftness of a cougar and shoved Thann to the ground a split second before an arrow whistled through the air. A second arrow was aimed at Quiet Thunder, but he dropped to the ground, rolled, and fired his rifle. The arrow disappeared into the deep shadows of the forest, but Quiet Thunder's bullet chewed bark next to the Shoshone, showering splinters. The young Indian howled and took off running.

As the other Shoshone tried to fit another arrow to his bow, Quiet Thunder worked the lever of his Winchester and fired. His haste spoiled his aim, but the bullet ripped the Shoshone's upper arm. The Indian let out a wild scream and ran after his partner into the forest.

"I guess they won't be back," Thann said.

"Not today," Quiet Thunder said. "Are you all right, Thann?"

"Thanks to you, I am. If you hadn't given me that shove, I'd probably be dead right now, or close to it. Thanks."

Quiet Thunder grinned. "You would have done the same for me." Quiet Thunder studied Thann. "You are growing up. I hardly knew you at first sight."

"Well, it's been four years, Quiet Thunder. You're growing up, too."

"We will be fifteen grasses soon. Three more grasses and you will go to soldier-coat school, and I will be old enough to be a warrior."

Thann grinned. "Well, I hope when you earn your feather, it will be when you've killed a Crow or Shoshone in battle, and not a white soldier."

Quiet Thunder did not comment.

Thann looked back toward the fort. "Well, my friend, it's time to go. Pa only allows me to hunt in these woods as long as I'm back when he tells me to be. I'm so glad we were both here today...thank you again for saving my life."

"Best friends are supposed to take care of each other."

"I wish we were brothers, Quiet Thunder."

Quiet Thunder looked into Thann's eyes for a long moment, then said, "I have learned how to become blood brothers. It is the Indian way, but it is real."

"You mean you and I could become real blood brothers?"

"Yes. We do it by mixing the blood from our wrists. It is done with an owl feather in between. The feather seals the brotherhood forever. Laughing Horse will give me one if I ask." Quiet Thunder paused, then said, "Are you afraid to cut yourself so we can be blood brothers?"

"Of course not. Let's do it."

Quiet Thunder touched his fingertips to his temple. "I have an idea, Thann."

"Yes?"

"Let us meet here at this spot on our birthday when the sun is highest."

"All right. June twenty-fifth at noon."

On June 25, just before noon, Quiet Thunder swung onto his pinto and trotted out of the village. Soon he reached the edge of the woods and slid from his pinto's back. He proceeded along a sun-dappled path, carrying his carbine in one hand and an owl feather in the other. The pungent scent of pine wafted in the gentle breeze.

Quiet Thunder reached the spot where he and his friend were to meet. It took only seconds for Thann to appear.

The two youths gripped each other's forearms, then Thann said, "Pa knows I'm meeting you here, but he won't let me come after this. He thinks it's becoming too dangerous."

"I understand," Quiet Thunder said.

They moved to a more secluded spot and sat down cross-legged, facing each other. Quiet Thunder placed the owl feather in his lap and told Thann to pull out his hunting knife. Quiet Thunder showed him the exact place to cut his wrist and explained that the cut did not have to be long, only enough for it to bleed freely.

They made the small incisions, and when the blood welled up, Quiet Thunder placed the owl feather against his bleeding wrist, then held it so Thann could press his cut to his.

When they were finished with the ceremony, the owl feather was buried in the earth between them, and the transaction was complete.

"Blood brothers forever, Thann," Quiet Thunder said.

"Yes, Quiet Thunder. Now we each carry a part of the other, no matter where we go."

They fell silent, then Thann said, "My mother says to tell your mother she misses her very much. She is hoping that one day there will be peace on these plains, and they can be together again."

"My mother speaks the same," Quiet Thunder said.

Thann rose to his feet.

"May Wakan Tanka keep you safe, my brother," Quiet Thunder said.

"And may God keep you safe, my brother…and…happy birthday."

Quiet Thunder smiled. "This is something Indians never say, my brother, but happy birthday to you, also."

When they had both taken several steps, they stopped and looked back.

"Blood brothers forever," Quiet Thunder said.

"Blood brothers forever," Thann echoed.

When Quiet Thunder got back to the village, his mother was standing and talking with a small group of women. After a few minutes, Gentle Fawn entered the teepee to find her son sitting on the dirt floor. She noted the cloth on his wrist.

"It is done?"

"Yes. We are blood brothers."

"I am glad." Gentle Fawn smiled briefly, then said, "My heart is in the ground for Andrea."

"Thann says she feels the same about you, Mother. She would ask Colonel Theron Tyler to bring her to see you, but she would be frowned upon, even as Thann's companions frowned upon him for being friendly to me. Only it would be worse because her husband is the fort's commandant."

Gentle Fawn nodded. "And our people would look at me as a traitor if I went to see her."

As time passed, a steady stream of settlers moved west. Many were Civil War veterans and their families. They came under vicious Indian attack in Dakota, Nebraska, Wyoming, Colorado, and Montana territories. Railroad crews, as well as bridge engineers, road builders, and emigrants, demanded protection by the army, and Washington responded by sending U.S. government commissioners to Fort Laramie on October 3, 1868.

Colonel Theron Tyler was seated at his desk going over government paperwork when the corporal who worked in the outer office tapped on the door. "Sorry to bother you, Colonel, but the commissioners are here."

Tyler rose from the desk and straightened his shirt collar. "Show them in."

Tyler figured the first man to enter must be the chief commissioner, so he extended his hand and said, "Welcome, Mr. Welton. I've been looking forward to your being here. And that goes for all of you."

James Welton smiled and shook Tyler's hand, then introduced the other members of the commission.

When all were seated, Welton said, "Colonel Tyler, I assume the necessary work has been done as I stated in my initial letter."

Tyler nodded. "Yes, sir. My men and those of the other forts in the territory have ridden under white flags to every Sioux, Cheyenne, and Arapaho village in a two-hundred-mile radius. Some sixty chiefs have said they will be here for the treaty discussion."

"What about Sitting Bull? He coming?"

"He's sending Gall in his place."

"What's the matter? Sitting Bull too good to sit down and negotiate with white men?"

"I have no idea why he isn't coming, Mr. Welton. He didn't give a reason. I'd say we ought to be glad he's at least sending his top war chief."

"Mmmm." Welton rubbed his ample chin. "And what about Red Cloud? He coming?"

"Said he would."

"But will he?"

"Mr. Welton," Tyler said, "let me tell you something about the Sioux...and the Cheyenne and Arapaho, for that matter. They are men of integrity."

"Integrity?" one of the other commissioners said. "Do you

call attacking wagon trains and stagecoaches and taking scalps of both men and women *integrity?*"

Tyler tried to remain calm. "Mr. Matthews, the Indians are fighting for their very existence. Their method of fighting may not fit our way of fighting, but when these Indians give their word on something, they will die before they break it."

He looked at the chief commissioner once more and said, "To answer your question, sir, yes. Red Cloud has said he will be here for the meeting, so I can guarantee you that unless he's sick or dead, he will be here."

"Well, he and Sitting Bull seem to be the top hogs at the trough," Welton said, "so I just want to make sure Red Cloud's coming, especially since Sitting Bull won't be here."

The next day, late in the afternoon, Indian chiefs and their escorts began arriving at Fort Laramie. They reported in at the gate, then set up their camps on the meadow. By sundown, every chief who had said he would attend the meeting had arrived.

On the morning of October 5, 1868, the meeting was held on the parade ground within the stockade walls. Chief Red Cloud sat in the center of the front row, with Sub-Chief Crazy Horse on his right. To his left was Gall, who led the Hunkpapa Sioux in fighting prowess. Although Sitting Bull was looked upon by all the Plains Indians as the greatest battle strategist among them, he had never been known to engage in combat. Next to Gall was Arapaho Chief Two Suns, and next to Crazy Horse was the venerable Cheyenne Chief Bear Killer.

Every chief and sub-chief in attendance looked to Red Cloud as their unofficial leader. They knew he had a strong distrust of the whites and would not be misled.

When it was time to start the meeting, Colonel Tyler introduced Welton, explaining that he and the other commissioners were sent by Washington as official representatives of the United States government.

Welton carefully laid out the terms of the treaty, watching Red Cloud without looking directly at him. As the Oglala leader listened, it was evident to him that the white men would lay claim to land wherever their railroad tracks ran and would confiscate land throughout the vast territory belonging to the tribes represented at the meeting.

Red Cloud's blood began to heat up. Gall and Crazy Horse noted his heavy breathing and the scarlet flush crawling up his neck.

Suddenly Red Cloud stood, breaking into Welton's words. "Just a moment, James Welton! I have listened to you tell us about all the land you plan to take from us, but I have not heard a word about what your government plans to give us in return."

A low murmur fanned through the Indians, and soldiers along the wall tensed.

Welton cleared his throat. "Well, ah...you are Chief Red Cloud, right?"

Red Cloud nodded.

"Chief, we are prepared to promise that white men will not invade your villages nor interfere with your mode of life. You will be allowed to—"

"Allowed? You are setting yourselves up as our superiors? You white men are going to *allow* us certain privileges while you steal our land? How can you not interfere with the way we live if you take our land? We cannot grow our crops and hunt our game if white eyes occupy it!"

The murmur grew louder.

Colonel Tyler rose from his chair and stepped up beside Welton. "Chief Red Cloud, I have no authority over these commissioners. But may I request that you hear Mr. Welton's entire proposal, then ask him any questions you like."

"This is acceptable, Colonel," Red Cloud said, "if James

Welton will answer one question for me right now."

Tyler turned to Welton, who rubbed a nervous hand over his face. "Yes, of course, Chief," Welton said.

"You seek safety for white eyes who settle on our land or make passage through it. You expect us to watch while white eyes take more. This happened many years ago to our Indian brothers in the East and in Texas. Before they knew it, they were herded like cattle onto reservations and robbed, not only of their land, but of their freedom. My question is this: Do you have the same plans for the Sioux, Cheyenne, and Arapaho as your greedy white brothers did for the Delaware, the Mohicans, the Seminoles, the Shawnees, the Cherokees, the Comanches, and many other tribes I could name?"

Welton's features took on a hard cast. "You must sit down and allow me to finish the terms of the treaty."

"You have not answered my question!" Red Cloud said.

"Chief Red Cloud, please…one thing at a time. I—"

"Colonel Tyler," Red Cloud said, "this Oglala chief has deep respect for you. You have shown yourself to be an honest man. I wish no ill will between us. But this James Welton—how do white men say it?—beats around the bush. This chief knows when he is being deceived."

"Now, just a minute!" Welton said. "I take offense at your remarks, Chief. All I want to do is finish presenting the terms of the proposed treaty. There is no need for you to—"

"All I am asking, James Welton," cut in Red Cloud, "is that you give me and all of my brother Indians an answer to the question."

Welton's face grew pale. "Well, I…ah…"

"That is answer enough!" Red Cloud said, rising to his feet. "Red Cloud will go now! White eyes government leaders speak with forked tongues like rattlesnakes! For this we will give you war!"

Within a week, the three mighty Indian nations were on the warpath.

SEVENTEEN

———◆———

At sunset on Quiet Thunder's sixteenth birthday, Gentle Fawn stood at the edge of the village and watched as two dots on the horizon grew larger. Quiet Thunder and Crazy Horse had been gone since early morning.

When they were within two hundred yards, Quiet Thunder waved to her, and somehow Gentle Fawn knew that her son had done it.

In a moment she could make out a furry object across the pinto's back. "Yes!" she said in a half-whisper. "He killed him a wolf."

Laughing Horse and White Wing came up beside her. "Do you see it?" Gentle Fawn said.

Laughing Horse squinted, then opened his eyes wide. "A wolf!"

"I knew he would do it before the day was over," White Wing said.

The villagers formed a large welcoming committee, Chief Red Cloud among them. When the riders came within thirty yards, a cheer went up.

As Quiet Thunder and Crazy Horse pulled rein, the crowd noted that the right forepaw had been severed and now hung on a leather thong around Quiet Thunder's neck.

After Red Cloud had publicly commended Quiet Thunder for his magnificent kill, and the crowd had dissipated, Gentle Fawn embraced her son. "Your father would be so proud of you, and your mother *is* so proud of you!"

"He did it with one shot, Gentle Fawn," Crazy Horse said.

Gentle Fawn opened her hand and offered the silver medallion. "Your father and I promised you that when you made your kill at sixteen grasses, you could wear John Stranger's medallion. Your uncle made a hole in it."

Quiet Thunder smiled at Crazy Horse and lifted the thong over his head, untied the knot, and strung the medallion next to the wolf's paw.

"John Stranger," Quiet Thunder said, "wherever you are, I want you to know that I will wear this medallion proudly."

In May 1870, at the age of seventeen, Thann Tyler finished high school with top grades. Two weeks later he left Fort Laramie with an army wagon train going east. He was enrolled at West Point, where he would follow the tradition of his family and prepare for a military career.

For the rest of the year, and into the next, Crazy Horse personally trained his nephew in every tactic of war. In the summer of 1871, four days after Quiet Thunder turned eighteen, Crazy Horse took him into battle against a column of soldiers from Fort Clark. Quiet Thunder made his first kill.

As Crazy Horse's warriors rode back toward the village carrying their dead and wounded, Quiet Thunder remembered Thann Tyler's words at their chance meeting in the forest: *I hope when you earn your feather, it will be when you have killed a Crow or a Shoshone in battle, and not a white soldier.*

The next morning, in a special ceremony, Chief Red Cloud

placed a large eagle feather under Quiet Thunder's headband and pronounced him a Sioux warrior. Gentle Fawn wiped her tears and wished Fire Eagle could see what a wonderful son he had produced.

In October, Crazy Horse led an attack on an army wagon train headed for Fort Laramie carrying guns, ammunition, and supplies. It was hard for Quiet Thunder to be part of the attack because of the Tylers, but he was brave and adept in combat, and he was fast becoming Crazy Horse's right-hand man.

Crazy Horse's band of Oglalas left the soldiers sprawled on the ground and took the horses and wagons. In the wagons were a hundred repeater rifles and plenty of ammunition.

By the time Quiet Thunder turned twenty, he had distinguished himself on the battlefield. When the war parties returned after their battles, much was said among the warriors about Quiet Thunder's courage under fire. Quiet Thunder was matched in fighting prowess only by the man who had trained him. Uncle and nephew made a powerful team and often fought side by side.

Three hundred Sioux warriors and as many soldiers fought a fierce battle near Fort Clark on August 2, 1873. Though many Sioux were cut down, the soldiers were driven back to the fort, dragging their wounded and leaving their dead. Quiet Thunder had killed six soldiers.

When the Oglala warriors returned to their village, Crazy Horse gave his report to Red Cloud, making sure the chief understood Quiet Thunder's role in the fight.

The next morning, Red Cloud called a special assembly. Quiet Thunder stood looking at the ground while Crazy Horse—at Red Cloud's request—told of Quiet Thunder's exploits the previous day. His fellow warriors cheered the loudest.

Gentle Fawn stood with her mother and wept for joy as Chief Red Cloud made her son a sub-chief, the youngest Oglala warrior to ever be so honored.

On September 22, 1873, Colonel Theron Tyler was crossing the parade ground to check on his horse's reshoeing. Several banks of high white clouds floated across the sky, and though the sun was shining, the air was taking on an autumn feel. Tyler was almost to the blacksmith shack when a corporal stationed at the gate approached him.

"Colonel, sir! The wagon train we're expecting from Fort Abraham Lincoln is coming in!"

Tyler smiled. "The way the Indians are hitting our supply trains, it's almost a miracle when one gets through. Thank you for letting me know."

"Well, sir, you need to come look."

"What do you mean?"

"It's your son, sir."

"Thann...here?"

"Yes, sir."

"Well, what're we waiting for? C'mon!"

As the colonel and the corporal approached the gate, the wagons were already rolling into the fort, and Thann was on the ground, leading his horse toward his father.

Theron hugged his son and then held him at arm's length. "When you left for West Point, you were still a wet-nosed kid! But look at you!" Thann had the same thick dark hair and blue eyes as his father.

"You don't look a day older, Pa!"

"Don't look too close at my hair, Son. You'll see some gray sneaking in."

"Hadn't noticed. How's Ma?"

"She's fine, Son. But she's going to be even better when she sees you! C'mon."

As father and son walked briskly toward the colonel's quarters, soldiers who knew Thann called out their hellos.

"Thann, your letter said you were assigned to a unit at Fort Rice, Dakota Territory. Why are you here?"

"I'll explain it to you and Ma as soon as I've given her a big hug," Thann said.

The colonel stepped ahead and opened the door. "Andrea…!"

"Yes, darling?" came her quick reply from the bedroom.

"I've got somebody out here who wants to give you a hug!"

"What? Who?"

Theron didn't answer. Both men waited for her to appear in the hallway.

"Thann!" Andrea clung to her son, crying for joy. Finally she wiped at her tears and said, "You sneaky little scamp! Why didn't you tell us you were coming?"

"I like surprises."

"Me too, but not the kind that make my heart stop! Theron, look at this boy. He's all grown up!"

"Not so much that I don't need Ma's cooking!" Thann said.

Andrea laughed and hugged him again. "The last your father and I knew, you were going to Fort Rice. Why—how—?"

"I'll explain that if you've got some cookies or something. I haven't eaten for about seven hours."

"Cookies I have, and it won't take long to heat up the leftover soup we had at lunch. Come on into the kitchen."

Thann and his father sat down at the table while Andrea worked at the cupboard and stove.

"What's happened is this," Thann said. "I was assigned to the Seventh Cavalry at Fort Rice. Pa, you probably know the Seventh has been at Fort Abraham Lincoln for quite some time.

Well, Fort Rice is just thirty miles south of Fort Lincoln on the Missouri River. That's why I was able to latch on to the wagon train. I've been assigned to a division of the Seventh Cavalry under the command of Lieutenant Colonel George Custer."

"Ah, yes," Theron said, rubbing his chin. "They call him Armstrong Custer, don't they?"

"I think that's mainly his wife, Libbie, and his brother, Tom, a lieutenant in the same division. Anyway, I'm in Custer's division."

Theron raised a finger. "Isn't this Custer the one who made brevet Brigadier General in the Civil War at the age of twenty-three?"

"Right."

"Then he was court-martialed in '67 for a string of offenses?"

"He was court-martialed for leaving Fort Wallace without permission from his superiors, and for excessive cruelty and illegal conduct when in a fit of anger—and without authority from his commanding officer—he ordered his men to shoot and kill soldiers he caught deserting."

"Was he convicted?" Andrea asked.

"Convicted and sentenced to a year's suspension from the army without pay. He's back in good standing now. General Phil Sheridan took up for him, reminding Washington that Custer was a hero in several Civil War battles."

"So you've been assigned to Custer's division," Theron said with a sigh.

"I'm not real happy about it, Pa. Custer's still more or less a rebel."

"Can't you request assignment to another division of the Seventh, Son?" Andrea asked.

"Not right now. You see, I haven't explained that I was able to come here and spend a few days with you because Colonel Custer's division is on an expedition along the Yellowstone River in Montana Territory. I'm supposed to meet up with them in ten days." Thann paused, then added, "As soon as we return to Fort Rice—and the proper opportunity presents itself—I'm going to ask for a transfer to another division."

"I'd say that would be the best thing to do, Son," Theron said.

Andrea placed a bowl of soup and some bread before Thann as he said, "Heard anything of Quiet Thunder?"

"No, we haven't," Andrea said. "It's been so long since I've seen Gentle Fawn."

"Well, in a sense, I've heard about your friend," Theron said. "I haven't mentioned it to your mother. Anytime Quiet Thunder or Gentle Fawn is mentioned, she gets melancholy."

Andrea hunched her shoulders and sighed.

"Quiet Thunder has become somewhat of a legend. As far as I know, none of my men have encountered him, but many soldiers of the other forts have gone up against him. Your blood brother is quite the warrior, from what I hear."

"I don't doubt it," Thann said. "He was always good at whatever he did."

Thann wolfed down the food and told his mother it was the best he'd eaten and always would be. Then he said, "I think before I leave for Montana I'll ride over to Red Cloud's village. I want to see Quiet Thunder."

"Oh, Thann, you can't go to that village! It's too dangerous!"

"Your mother's right, Son," Theron said. "Things are too hot in these parts for a man in army uniform to ride up to a Sioux village. They'd probably shoot first and ask questions later."

Thann set his jaw in the way they had seen since he was a child. "I appreciate your concern for me," he said, "but if I ride up to the Oglala village alone, unarmed, with a white flag, they certainly wouldn't start shooting."

"Son, I can understand your wanting to see Quiet Thunder after all these years, but it isn't worth risking your life."

"Well, if it really meant a risk, it would be worth it, Pa.

Quiet Thunder saved my life once. I owe him. But if I ride over there as I just stated, I'm sure—"

"Okay, okay," the elder Tyler said, throwing up his hands. "We'll work out a compromise. But you can't go riding out of this fort unarmed. There are too many miles between here and the village. Tell you what. There's a patrol that scouts the area just beyond the east side of the forest. You can ride with the patrol to within rock-throwing distance of the village. They'll wait for you. It's that way, or so help me, I'll take you down and sit on you to prevent you from going."

Thann laughed. "He hasn't lost an ounce of stubbornness, has he, Ma?"

"Same as you," she said with a chuckle.

The sun was just rising as Thann removed the gun and holster from his belt and handed it to Lieutenant Efram Smith, leader of the patrol. The other thirteen men looked toward the village, which lay a hundred yards to the east.

The patrol had brought two white flags. As a trooper handed one to Thann, he said, "Looks to me like ol' Red Cloud has beefed up his army. There aren't usually that many horses in his corral."

"Could be they've got company from Sitting Bull's village, or some other one," Thann said. "Doesn't change anything. I'm going in there and find out if my friend is home."

Thann trotted his blaze-faced bay gelding toward the village. When he was within forty yards, a dozen or more warriors appeared, carrying their carbines. Their unfriendly faces gazed at him as he drew rein and raised his hand in a sign of peace.

"I am Lieutenant Thann Tyler. I am here to see Quiet Thunder."

The warriors looked toward the army patrol in the distance.

The warrior who seemed to be the leader stepped forward. "Quiet Thunder very busy. Many Hunkpapa here. Sitting Bull and Gall here. Many warriors. Women. Children. You leave now, soldier coat."

"Please. I am a long-time friend of Quiet Thunder. Just have one of these warriors tell him Thann Tyler is here. I know he will want to see me."

"You go now. We honor white flag, but only if you go *now!*"

Just then Laughing Horse passed by and recognized Thann. His ears picked up the warrior's words. Before the young lieutenant could speak again, Laughing Horse brushed past the warrior and said, "Thann Tyler! Welcome!"

"Thank you, Laughing Horse," Thann said. "I have come to see Quiet Thunder, but this warrior has told me to leave."

Laughing Horse turned and fixed the Indian with steady eyes. "This soldier coat is blood brother to Quiet Thunder, Walking Bird. If you send him away and Quiet Thunder learns of it, you will be in big trouble."

Walking Bird stepped aside without another word.

The Oglala village was a beehive of activity. Oglala children played happily with their Hunkpapa guests. The young unmarried men and women were collected in groups, talking and laughing, and women were clustered together, as were the men. Sitting Bull was speaking with Red Cloud and some of the aged warriors of both tribes.

Quiet Thunder sat in front of his teepee with Crazy Horse and Hunkpapa War Chief Gall, discussing the construction of another new fort some forty miles south of the village. Anger flashed in Gall's eyes as he said, "This fort means more soldiers and guns to punish us for attacking wagon trains. We become outnumbered more all the time. Our weapons are not like theirs.

We must find a way to take weapons. We must—"

Quiet Thunder and Crazy Horse turned to see what had captured Gall's attention.

"Thann Tyler!" Quiet Thunder leaped to his feet and embraced his blood brother.

Many of the Indians scowled and began to murmur. Quiet Thunder heard them and ran his gaze over their faces before saying, "This man is Thann Tyler, Quiet Thunder's blood brother!"

Those words changed most frowns to smiles and hushed the murmuring. Crazy Horse's expression had not changed. As Quiet Thunder introduced Thann to War Chief Gall, Crazy Horse slipped away.

Thann's stay was politely short. Under the gaze of hundreds of Indians, he and Quiet Thunder walked to the edge of the village and said goodbye. Then Thann mounted his horse and rode slowly toward the army patrol waiting under a white flag.

Thann had ridden about twenty yards when he drew rein and looked back. Quiet Thunder had been waiting for him to do that. A warm smile curved his lips as he said, "Blood brothers forever."

Thann smiled back. "Blood brothers forever, Quiet Thunder."

CHAPTER
EIGHTEEN

As Quiet Thunder threaded his way back through the crowd, he noticed his uncle coming toward him, a look of displeasure on his face.

"Quiet Thunder," Crazy Horse said, "it is not good to become too attached to white eyes."

"You speak of Thann?"

"Yes."

"Thann is not white eyes, Uncle. He is blood brother."

"My nephew should not forget that white men are making plans to take our land from us."

"Thann would not steal our land. He is blood brother."

"But he is part of white-eyes army who kill Indians and want to make us live as trapped animals."

Quiet Thunder scowled. "I wear war paint and kill white men, but Thann is still my friend...and my faithful blood brother. Neither of us wish to kill each other's people, but we must be loyal to our own, so we fight and kill our enemies on the battlefield."

Crazy Horse's mouth pulled into a thin line. "Yes, we must be loyal to our own people. White eyes are enemies of Sioux. If my nephew came face to face with his blood brother on the battlefield, would he kill him?"

Quiet Thunder gave his uncle a wintry stare, then turned quickly to walk away. He collided with a young Hunkpapa maiden and reached out to steady her.

"Oh, I am sorry!"

"It is all right," the girl said, and smiled.

"I have not met you before," Quiet Thunder said.

"No, we have not met, but I know who you are. You are Quiet Thunder, son of the great warrior, Fire Eagle, whose spirit walked away to join the Sky People. I…I have watched you many times when our people have been together."

Quiet Thunder guessed that she was not more than eighteen grasses. The last time the Oglalas and the Hunkpapas had been together, she would have seemed too young for his attention. It was then he saw a younger girl. "And who might you be?" he asked.

"This is Star Flower, my littler sister, and I am Night Star, daughter of one of Sitting Bull's sub-chiefs, Lame Elk," the older girl said.

Quiet Thunder nodded courteously "I am very happy to meet you Night Star…and you, Star Flower. I know much of your father, Lame Elk. He is a great warrior."

"Yes. And I have heard much of Quiet Thunder of late. He also is a great warrior."

Quiet Thunder looked toward the ground.

"I congratulate Quiet Thunder on being made sub-chief at such a young age," Night Star said. "If your father were alive, I am sure he would be very proud of you, and I am sure that your mother takes pride in such a fine son."

"I would like to believe so," Quiet Thunder said.

Night Star wore a buckskin dress with beads at the neck and cuffs. The dress fell to her ankles just above moccasins trimmed with beads matching those on her dress. She wore a necklace of rawhide dyed red with hardened clay balls strung on it.

"Night Star is very beautiful," Quiet Thunder said.

"Does…does she have an intended?"

"No, she does not."

Star Flower smiled to herself. She had seen many a young man show great interest in her older sister. But not like this. Quiet Thunder's eyes gave him away. Little sister knew what was going on in big sister's heart, for Night Star had pointed out Quiet Thunder many times since they had arrived at the Oglala village. It was no accident that Quiet Thunder had bumped into Night Star. She had been watching him closely all day.

Quiet Thunder cleared his throat nervously. "It would be this warrior's great pleasure to escort Night Star along the creek bank this evening."

Night Star smiled and said, "It would be Night Star's great pleasure to be accompanied along the creek bank with the great warrior, Quiet Thunder."

That evening, Quiet Thunder was introduced to Night Star's parents. Both Lame Elk and Pale Moon told him they had heard much of his exploits on the battlefield and expressed their pleasure at meeting him.

As Quiet Thunder and Night Star strolled along the tree-lined bank of the creek, he showed her the silver medallion he wore around his neck and told her of the mysterious John Stranger who had saved his life and that of his mother. Night Star said that maybe someday Wakan Tanka would bring them together again.

During the next several days, Quiet Thunder was involved in the conferences during the day, but when evening came, he was walking along the creek bank with Night Star.

The Hunkpapas had been at the Oglala village for nearly two weeks when Sitting Bull and Red Cloud finally finished their business. The Hunkpapas would leave the next morning.

That night, as Quiet Thunder and Night Star walked, they stopped at a spot where the creek made a slight bend and a fallen pine offered a place to sit. The silvery crescent moon was almost insignificant compared to the great canopy of stars overhead.

Instead of wearing her hair in braids that evening, Night Star had brushed it out and let it fall in wavy swirls down her back. The breeze toyed with it, making her more alluring than ever.

A wolf howled somewhere in the night, its mournful wail elongated by the breeze. When the howl died out, Quiet Thunder turned and said, "The wolf sounds very lonely...just as Quiet Thunder will be when Night Star is not here."

A second wolf howl came from the opposite direction, sounding as forlorn and lonely as the first.

"His mate sounds lonely too," Night Star said. "Even as Night Star will be when she is not with Quiet Thunder."

"The male wolf will be happy only when the two of them are together," he said, squeezing her hand. "It is the same with Quiet Thunder, because he has fallen in love with Night Star."

Night Star gently pulled her hand free and rose to her feet. She looked down at the creek for a moment, then turned to face the tall man who now stood behind her, waiting for her response.

Night Star's eyes grew misty as she silently spread both hands over her heart and gradually opened them like a flower responding to the rays of the morning sun.

Elated, Quiet Thunder folded her in his strong arms and held her close for a long moment. When they parted, the stars seemed to have deserted the surface of the rippling creek and settled in her eyes.

"There are words in the wind, Quiet Thunder," Night Star said, "and I have heard them. I have heard them each evening as we have walked together. I have heard them when lying on my bed in my father's teepee after being with you. I have awakened in the night and heard them speak to me, telling me that my heart belongs only to Quiet Thunder. And I now tell you, not only with my hands but with my lips. My heart belongs only to Quiet Thunder, and it always will."

Quiet Thunder stroked her long, silky hair as he held her tightly and said, "And the wind has other words, my beautiful one. They say that Quiet Thunder's heart belongs only to Night Star, and it always will."

At sunrise the next morning, the aroma of roasting venison filled the air as the children—who always ate last—finished their breakfast. While the Hunkpapa men loaded their gear on horses and travois, preparing for their all-day journey home, Pale Moon and Night Star talked to Gentle Fawn and White Wing and a few other women of both tribes. Star Flower was playing with the children nearby.

Red Cloud and Sitting Bull were talking, and Crazy Horse and Gall compared the rifles they had taken from army wagon trains. Quiet Thunder passed by them. Gall nodded a greeting, but Crazy Horse glanced at him and looked away.

Quiet Thunder walked straight toward Lame Elk who, with the help of Wind Hawk, was loading his travois with bedding and other items. When Quiet Thunder drew near, both men smiled and greeted him.

"Wind Hawk was just telling me about the time you saved his life by killing a Crow who was about to shoot him in the back. You were only fourteen grasses at the time?"

"Yes, this is true. Please forgive my interrupting, Lame Elk, but I would like to talk to you in private before you leave."

"You may do so now," Wind Hawk said. "There is work to do at my teepee."

When they were alone Lame Elk said, "What is it you wish to discuss with me, Quiet Thunder?"

"It is not in me to talk around a subject before getting to it, Lame Elk," Quiet Thunder said. "You have observed that Night Star and I have spent much time together these several evenings."

"Yes."

"I am asking Night Star's father for her hand in marriage. She and Quiet Thunder have pledged their love to each other forever. Quiet Thunder loves Lame Elk's daughter more than he loves life. He would be much honored to be a son-in-law of Lame Elk and Pale Moon."

Lame Elk let a smile curve his lips as he said, "It would be an honor to have Fire Eagle's son as my son-in-law."

"Quiet Thunder's heart thanks you, Lame Elk."

"Like any father, I want my daughter to be happy. You and Night Star have discussed a time for the wedding?"

"We have not. Quiet Thunder has not yet asked Night Star for her hand. He felt it wise to ask her father first."

"I see. So if Lame Elk had refused her hand, there would be less disappointment for Night Star."

"Yes."

The stalwart older warrior said, "Quiet Thunder will make a good husband to Night Star. Go. Ask her to be your squaw."

Quiet Thunder's pulse raced as he hurried across the village to where Night Star stood with her mother and the other women. Night Star saw him and smiled. He motioned for her to come to him, and Night Star excused herself.

"Yes, Quiet Thunder?"

"Would you walk with me to our favorite spot by the creek?"

When they reached the fallen pine, Quiet Thunder sat her down and stood over her, smiling.

"What is it?" she asked.

"Quiet Thunder just spoke with Night Star's father. Quiet Thunder asked Lame Elk for his daughter's hand in marriage."

"So soon? I—"

"Lame Elk gave Quiet Thunder permission to marry his

daughter. What does his daughter say?"

Night Star's eyes filled with tears. "She says yes! She will marry Quiet Thunder!"

They embraced, and as Night Star remained in his arms, she asked, "How soon does Night Star become the squaw of Quiet Thunder?"

"I am thinking seven moons."

Her eyes widened as she pulled back and looked into his eyes. "Seven moons?"

"Too soon?"

"Oh, no!"

"Then let us go and let it be known to all."

Before going to Red Cloud—who as chief of the groom's tribe would make the public announcement—the happy couple went to Gentle Fawn and Pale Moon. Both mothers had seen it coming. Gentle Fawn told Night Star that she was very proud of her son and full of joy that he had chosen such a lovely young woman for his squaw.

Red Cloud announced that the wedding was set for a week from that day. Sitting Bull discussed it with Gall and the sub-chiefs, and it was decided that all the Hunkpapas would stay for the wedding.

Three days before the wedding, Quiet Thunder and Night Star were sitting on their fallen pine tree when Night Star noticed a sadness come over Quiet Thunder.

"Something is wrong, my love. What troubles you?"

"Night Star," he said softly, "I have not told you of my blood brother."

"You have a blood brother? A *real* blood brother?"

"Yes. He is not Indian. He is white."

"White?"

"Yes. His name is Thann Tyler. He is a soldier coat. Thann was here the day you and I met. He—"

"Oh, yes! I saw you talking to a soldier coat. He came to the village with a white flag. And there were more soldier coats who waited for him in the distance."

"That was him."

"And you wish he could attend our wedding."

"Yes. But I do not even know where he is. When he was here that day, he said he was being sent to Montana."

Quiet Thunder told her the story of how he and Thann Tyler were both born at the same place on the same day and how their friendship grew so strong that they became blood brothers. "Does it bother Night Star that her husband-to-be is blood brother to a white man?"

Night Star looked into his eyes and said, "I am sure Thann Tyler is everything you say he is, my love. Though it surprised me at first, I understand now. No, it does not bother me. I hope someday I can meet your blood brother."

"That would make me very happy," Quiet Thunder said.

Night Star thought she still read sadness in his eyes. "Is something else bothering my love?"

"Yes. It is my uncle. His hatred toward whites consumes him. There was a time when Crazy Horse was friendly toward Thann and his parents. He feels this no more. On the day you and I met, when Thann was here, Crazy Horse spoke ill of my relationship with him. He has barely spoken to me since."

"I am sorry," Night Star said, taking his hand. "Your uncle is a great and mighty warrior. You must admire him for that and try to get along, since you must fight together."

On October 7, 1873, the wedding took place with medicine man Laughing Horse officiating. Both Red Cloud and Sitting Bull took part in the ceremony to show their approval of the young couple.

A wedding feast had been prepared by the women of both tribes, with Gentle Fawn and Pale Moon overseeing it. The feast had barely started when a lone Cheyenne rider galloped into the village. Chief Bear Killer and a small band of Cheyenne had been cornered by soldier coats from Fort Clark in retaliation for a wagon train they had wiped out three days earlier.

Quiet Thunder kissed his bride and galloped away beside his uncle, as both Oglala and Hunkpapa warriors hastened to help the Cheyenne. Night Star watched her husband ride off to battle and prayed to Wakan Tanka for his safety.

In early January, Night Star surprised her husband by telling him they were going to have a papoose. The young warrior was very happy and rushed all over the village to announce it.

On August 12, both Gentle Fawn and White Wing served as midwives as Night Star gave birth to a beautiful baby girl. The parents named her Blue Sky.

On October 3, Lieutenant Thann Tyler arrived at Fort Laramie, once again surprising his parents. His last letter had come in August, telling them he was still in Custer's division of the Seventh Cavalry and that they were leaving the Black Hills in western Dakota Territory and returning to Fort Abraham Lincoln.

Thann had traveled with an army wagon train carrying supplies, guns, and ammunition to forts in central Wyoming. He would return with the same train in four days. Before he did, he wanted to see his blood brother once more.

At dawn two days later, Laughing Horse bathed Blue Sky's tiny fevered body in cold water. He had wrapped her in wet leaves from a prairie plant and was chanting as he tended her.

The parents, along with grandmother Gentle Fawn and great-grandmother White Wing, huddled together, looking on. Blue Sky had been sick for three days, and so far Laughing Horse had been unable to help her.

Quiet Thunder had been ordered by Chief Red Cloud to deliver a detailed message to Arapaho Chief Two Suns some thirty miles to the northwest. He was to take along an escort of nine warriors and leave at sunrise.

"I will go to Chief Red Cloud and tell him my journey to Chief Two Suns' village must wait until Blue Sky is improved," Quiet Thunder told Laughing Horse.

Laughing Horse looked up from the sick baby. "You must go. Red Cloud needs the message delivered to Two Suns today. Only you has he trusted with it."

"Laughing Horse is right, my husband," Night Star said. "You must go. Wakan Tanka will watch over Blue Sky while you are gone."

Quiet Thunder knew his chief had honored him with such a mission, so he gave in, saying he would do his best to be back before dark.

The sun was setting as Quiet Thunder and his escort returned, skirting the northeast edge of the great forest not far from the village. They topped a hill, dropped into a shallow meadow, then climbed up a gentle slope. When they reached the crest, Wind Hawk, who rode beside Quiet Thunder, pointed.

Fifty yards ahead, five pintos were huddled by a white man kneeling beside an Oglala warrior. The white man's huge black gelding stood nearby. Two of the pintos had deer draped over their backs.

Quiet Thunder motioned for his warriors to follow and put

his horse to a gallop. When they pulled up, they recognized the warrior on the ground as Tall Bear. The others were White Antelope and War Hand.

The white man glanced at them over his shoulder and continued to work on Tall Bear.

"What has happened?" Quiet Thunder asked.

"We were hunting." White Antelope gestured toward the deer. "Three Shoshone braves came out of the woods over there and started shooting. When we fired in return, they rode back into the woods."

"Tall Bear took a bullet in his side, Quiet Thunder," War Hand said. "This white man came along and removed the bullet. He told us he is not a medical doctor, but that he has treated many bullet wounds."

War Hand saw the skepticism on the other warriors' faces. "Though he is a white man, White Antelope and I saw something in his eyes. It told us he is a friend."

The white man finished stitching up Tall Bear's wound, closed the small black bag next to him, and rose to his feet. Quiet Thunder and his warriors looked at him in awe when he reached his full height. They had never seen a man so tall. The man's right cheek bore twin jagged scars. He wore a well-trimmed mustache and his expressive eyes were the color of gunmetal.

The tall man spoke to White Antelope and War Hand. "I took out the bullet and sewed up the wound. Your medicine man should dress it again in a few days. Tell him to remove the stitches in ten days—ten moons."

Suddenly the man noticed Quiet Thunder's silver medallion on the thong around his neck. A smile lit up his face as he said, "I heard them call you Quiet Thunder."

"Yes."

"*Hohahe*, Quiet Thunder," he said, and offered his hand. "I see you wear a silver medallion that says, *The stranger that shall come from a far land.*"

Quiet Thunder's mouth went dry as he shook hands Indian style.

"Your mother must have spoken of me, Quiet Thunder. I am John Stranger."

CHAPTER

NINETEEN

———◆———

Quiet Thunder had lived for this day, but now he was speechless.

Stranger reached in his pocket and pulled out an identical medallion and held it up. "Just in case you're wondering if I'm who I say I am."

Quiet Thunder found his tongue. "There is no need for that, John Stranger. It is just that I have heard about you all of my life and have hoped that one day I could meet you. Now that it has happened, I find it hard to believe. Wakan Tanka has been good to cross our paths today."

Stranger placed his medical bag in a saddlebag, then turned and said, "Tall Bear must be taken to your village. I will be glad to carry him on my horse, if it's all right with you."

"Of course," Quiet Thunder said. "You must come to the village. My mother and grandmother will want to see you."

"I had that in mind," Stranger said with a grin. "I'm on a journey to help someone in need, but I have a little time to spare. Not long ago, I passed by the spot where the village used to be, intending to pay a visit, but I could tell by the way the grass had grown that you haven't lived there in a long time."

"It pleases me that you would do that, John Stranger," Quiet

Thunder said. "Yes, it has been many grasses since we lived there."

"How about Curly? How is he?"

"He is fine, only my grandfather, Laughing Horse, has changed Curly's name to Crazy Horse."

"Crazy Horse! I've heard much about that Oglala warrior. It'll be good to see him again."

Quiet Thunder hoped his uncle would treat John Stranger decently.

While Stranger carried the semiconscious Tall Bear on his horse, Quiet Thunder told him about Fire Eagle being killed, then said that he was married to Night Star, and that they had a baby girl named Blue Sky. He talked about little Blue Sky's fever.

John offered to look at her if Quiet Thunder and Night Star would like him to.

Night Star was carrying a pail of water from the creek when the warriors rode in at dusk. She set it down and ran toward them.

"Quiet Thunder, what happened?" Night Star said.

"Shoshones shot Tall Bear, but this man removed the bullet. Tall Bear will live because of him."

Night Star looked at the towering white man.

"You remember I told you about John Stranger?" Quiet Thunder said.

"Of course. You wear his medallion."

"Night Star, this is him."

"O John Stranger," Night Star said, "I owe you so much. If it were not for you, I would have no Quiet Thunder."

"I was just doing my duty, Night Star," Stranger said. "You don't owe me a thing."

"How is our baby?" Quiet Thunder asked.

"She is no better."

"John Stranger has offered to look at her."

"Oh, would you, John Stranger? I would be so grateful if you could help our little Blue Sky."

People stared at the white man as he walked through their village. Night Star picked up the pail of water on the way back and her husband took it from her hand. They were near the teepee when Red Cloud and Crazy Horse appeared. Stranger knew by Red Cloud's headdress that he was the chief. He did not recognize Crazy Horse.

"We just learned about Tall Bear," Red Cloud said as they came near and stopped. "War Hand told us this man removed the bullet."

Crazy Horse was studying John Stranger. It took him a few seconds to realize who he was. Stranger had flecks of silver in his dark hair, and he had picked up a pair of jagged twin scars on his right cheek.

"John Stranger," Quiet Thunder said, "this is our chief, Red Cloud."

Stranger took a step closer, and with a slight bow, touched the fingertips of his left hand to his forehead. *"Woyuonihan,"* he said. The Lakota word was used only to show the highest esteem for a chief.

"You are most welcome, John Stranger," Red Cloud said. "Red Cloud has heard much of you from Gentle Fawn and White Wing. Please accept his appreciation for what you did for Tall Bear."

"It was my pleasure." Then Stranger looked at the warrior standing next to the chief.

"John Stranger," Quiet Thunder said, "this is Crazy Horse, whom you knew as Curly."

Stranger read the hostility in Crazy Horse's eyes but smiled anyway and extended his hand. "I remember Curly well, though I didn't recognize him just now. He has grown up. We became friends in the short time I was in the village."

Crazy Horse's expression remained impassive, and he shook

Stranger's hand apathetically, Indian style, and mumbled, "It has been a long time."

Stranger ignored the warrior's coldness toward him and quickly explained to Red Cloud that he was on his way to look at Blue Sky.

Gentle Fawn was just coming out of the teepee to check on Night Star and the pail of water when she stopped in her tracks. The tall man had matured, but she would have known him anywhere. She rushed to meet them.

"Mother, do you remember this man?"

Tears filmed Gentle Fawn's eyes. "John Stranger! Wakan Tanka has brought you back to us!"

She forgot Lakota custom and embraced him. John hugged her in return, saying, "Gentle Fawn, it's so good to see you!"

Gentle Fawn suddenly realized what she had done and stepped back. "Oh, please forgive me, John Stranger. It is not for squaw to embrace a man who is not her husband."

John smiled. "There's nothing to forgive. I'm just so glad to—"

White Wing heard Stranger's name on her daughter's lips and came rushing from the teepee to greet him. A few moments later, inside the teepee, White Wing introduced John Stranger to Laughing Horse. The aging medicine man remembered him immediately and welcomed his offer to help little Blue Sky.

Stranger examined the baby, then turned to Quiet Thunder and asked for the small black bag from his saddlebags. When Quiet Thunder returned with it, Stranger requested that they leave him alone with the baby, saying he could work better that way.

By morning the fever was gone, and the little Indian girl was cooing and kicking her fat little legs. The parents were ecstatic, and Night Star wept for joy as she held Blue Sky in her arms.

Word spread that little Blue Sky's condition was greatly improved. Red Cloud appeared with the rest of the village at his back, except for Crazy Horse, and expressed his deepest gratitude for what the white man had done.

Stranger looked over the crowd and said loudly enough for all to hear, "I was only able to make Blue Sky well because of help from God in heaven and His Son, the Lord Jesus Christ. It is important that you understand that.

"I know many of you have heard of Jesus Christ. It is by His power that Blue Sky lives. He has power to deliver us from our bodily sicknesses, but more than that, He has power to deliver us from the sickness of our souls—the sickness of sin.

"There is a misunderstanding among you that Jesus Christ is the Saviour only of white men. This is not true. His book, which we call the Bible, says, 'God sent his only begotten Son into the world, that we might live through him.' That's *all* of us—white men, red men, and all peoples of the—"

There was a rustling among the crowd as Wind Hawk rushed up. "Please excuse, John Stranger, but there is someone here who wants to see Quiet Thunder."

All eyes turned to look at another white man. This one was in the uniform of the United States Army and had lieutenant's bars on his shoulders.

"Thann!" Quiet Thunder ran to meet his blood brother.

The crowd looked on as Quiet Thunder excitedly introduced Night Star and showed Thann the baby in her arms. He then introduced him to John Stranger. Thann knew the story of Stranger and the medallion, and he marveled that he had the good fortune to meet him at last.

Soon the people went back to the day's tasks, and the children were playing as usual. Night Star fed little Blue Sky and placed the sleepy baby in her crib.

"I tried to keep Wind Hawk from interrupting you, Mr. Stranger," Thann said, "but he insisted."

"That's because Wind Hawk knows Thann Tyler is Quiet Thunder's blood brother," Gentle Fawn said.

"Blood brothers?" John said. "You mean the cut wrists and the owl feather?"

"Yes," Quiet Thunder said. "You know so much about the Lakotas—our language and our customs. How is this?"

"Maybe we'll have time someday for me to explain it," Stranger said, "but right now I'm concerned with something more important." He turned to Gentle Fawn. "Do you remember way back there when Quiet Thunder was born, you promised me you would read the Bible the missionary gave you?"

Gentle Fawn blushed. "Yes, I remember."

"Do you still have that Bible?"

"I do."

"Have you read it?"

Gentle Fawn cleared her throat. "I have read it occasionally."

"Have you understood about the Lord Jesus and your need for Him?"

"I have thought a lot about what you told me. The things you were saying to all of us earlier were very familiar."

John Stranger looked at each face before he said, "The most important thing in this life is to be sure you are ready for the next one. This one is very short, the next one is forever...and you will either spend it in heaven or hell.

"Turn to Jesus Christ in repentance of your sin and He will save you. He will wash your sins away in His precious blood, place you in the family of God, and take you to heaven when you die."

"Mr. Stranger," Thann said, "I'm amazed that I would run onto you here and that you would be telling us this. We have a chaplain at Fort Abraham Lincoln who's been talking to me in exactly the same way. I've been thinking about it a lot. It's crossed my mind every time our Seventh Cavalry goes into battle—what if I should die today? Where would I be five seconds after I die?"

"The most important question you can ask yourself, Lieutenant," Stranger said.

Quiet Thunder spoke up. "I must confess something to my mother, and to you, John Stranger. Many times since I learned to read English as a boy, I have read the Bible in Mother's box when no one else was around. I let much time pass between my reading, because I found myself doubting the Lakota religion."

"That has been *my* problem," Gentle Fawn said. "I feel guilty when I question our religion."

"The true and living God of heaven did not make the religions, Gentle Fawn," Stranger said. "People make up religious formalities to try to please a holy God. But God's Book says we are saved by faith in Jesus Christ. His death was a substitution for our death. Then He came to life again to show His triumph over death, and if we believe this, we too can live forever with God."

When John Stranger saw that he had everyone's attention, he said, "Gentle Fawn, I would like you to get your Bible, and I will get mine."

With both Bibles open so everyone could see the pages, Stranger took them to Matthew's account of the crucifixion, burial, and resurrection.

Tears began to stream down Night Star's cheeks. With a quaver in her voice, she said, "I have never heard this before, John Stranger, but in spite of what I have been taught in the Lakota religion all my life, I know in my heart that what it says in this Bible is true. Jesus will save me right now if I ask Him. I know He will."

"He sure will, Night Star."

"My father is a Lakota medicine man," Gentle Fawn said, "and I love him. But like Night Star, I know deep in my heart that what you have shown us is true. There is a...shall I say, a *voice?* I do not hear it with my ears, but I hear it in my heart. The voice is saying, 'Gentle Fawn, open your heart to Jesus.'"

"That's the Holy Spirit of God speaking to you," Stranger said.

"Well, He's speaking to me too," Quiet Thunder said. "I love

my Lakota people and will continue to carry on their fight to keep
our land, but I will do it as a Christian. As you have shown us, John
Stranger, I want Jesus to wash away my sins in His blood."

"And so do I," Thann Tyler said. "I want my sins cleansed
by Jesus' blood, too."

"Then we will be blood brothers in another way, Thann,"
Quiet Thunder said.

White Wing stood up. Her hands were trembling. "John
Stranger," she said, "this is very difficult for me. My husband is
the Oglalas' religious leader. I...I must think this over. The missionary Paul Breland almost convinced me years ago, but
Laughing Horse became very angry when I told him I thought
the Christian way was right. I must ask you to excuse me."

Stranger watched her go, then said to the others, "I know
how difficult it is to turn from your religion to Jesus Christ, and
my heart is heavy for White Wing."

After each one had called on the Lord, Stranger encouraged
them to read the Bible and spend time every day in prayer. They
were thrilled with their newfound faith. Quiet Thunder held
Night Star's hand and looked around at the other bright faces.

"I have always thought of the stars in the heavens as the
shining faces of the Sky People," Night Star said. "Now that I
have learned the truth from the Bible, I believe the Sky People's
faces shine even brighter than the stars because they are so happy
to be up there with Jesus."

"That is a beautiful way to say it," Gentle Fawn said.

Stranger rose to his feet. "Well, I must be going. I have a
long ride yet to get to my destination."

The three Indians and Thann Tyler walked Stranger to his
horse. Then Quiet Thunder said, "John Stranger, how can we
ever thank you? Not only did you do wonderful things for us
many years ago, but today you have saved the life of our little Blue
Sky...and you have brought us to Jesus Christ. I find mere words
so frail."

"It is thanks enough for me to know I will meet you in heaven," Stranger said. With that, he gave the women and Thann Tyler each a silver medallion, then mounted up and rode away.

The new Christians spent the rest of the day in Quiet Thunder and Night Star's teepee, talking about their newfound faith.

As the sun began to set, the army patrol appeared at the edge of the village under a white flag. Thann bid the women goodbye, then Quiet Thunder walked with him to the edge of the village. When Thann reached his horse, he said, "Only God knows when we will meet again, Quiet Thunder. But one thing we know for sure. If we should not meet again in this life, we will be together in the next."

They embraced as the soldiers watched. Then Thann stepped into the stirrup and settled in his saddle. "Blood brothers forever, Quiet Thunder."

"In two ways, now," Quiet Thunder said. "Blood brothers forever."

A few days after Lieutenant Thann Tyler arrived back at Fort Abraham Lincoln, Custer's division of the Seventh Cavalry was relocated to Fort Supply in central Kansas. The Shawnees were on the warpath, and more troops were needed.

An hour after sunrise on a cool day in mid-October, Lieutenant Colonel George Armstrong Custer stood before his patrol unit of seventy-five men. Custer was tall and lean, with small wide-set blue eyes, bushy eyebrows, and a cleft in his chin. His curly shoulder-length hair and drooped handlebar mustache were a cornsilk shade of yellow. He wore a vivid red scarf knotted loosely about his throat in keeping with his label as the "dandy" of the Seventh Cavalry Regiment.

"Gentlemen," he said, "this scouting will be a four-day

jaunt. General Philip Sheridan wants us to go as far south as Wichita and see if the Shawnees are setting up any more war camps. If they are, that will mean they're planning more assaults on white towns and settlements."

At Custer's command, the cavalry mounted, and the long column rode south two-by-two out of Fort Supply. Captain Chick Hays rode next to Custer, and immediately behind them rode Lieutenants Thann Tyler and Royce Robins.

The first day out was uneventful. The platoon made camp on the banks of a small creek and rode out at sunrise the next morning. Late in the afternoon, they were approaching the Arkansas River at a spot twelve miles northwest of Wichita when the roar of guns echoed from the west.

Custer's head snapped around. White puffs of gunsmoke lifted skyward above a line of bare-branched cottonwoods. A quick glance through his binoculars showed him Indians and soldiers in battle just beyond the trees. The Indians were definitely Shawnees, and they outnumbered the soldiers. Custer commanded his men to follow him across the river.

They splashed across the Arkansas and galloped hard toward the cottonwoods. When the Shawnees saw Custer's troops, they wheeled their pintos and thundered away, heading west.

The platoon passed through the trees onto the meadow to find a grisly scene. Soldiers, about twenty of them, were scattered everywhere, their bodies bristling like porcupines with Shawnee arrows. Four Indians lay amongst them.

Custer saw the galloping Shawnees top a rise and disappear into a low spot. "After them!" he commanded.

They lost sight of the Shawnees several times during the pursuit over undulating land, but the Indians would appear again in a few seconds. Twenty minutes of hard riding brought the platoon into a low-lying meadow fringed by heavy brush.

"Where could they have gone, Colonel?" Captain Hays said, searching the panorama. "I saw them top the crest and ride in here. We were close enough they couldn't have reached the other crest all the way over there on the west side."

"I can't figure it either," Custer said, "but they sure aren't here."

"Looks to me like a good place for an ambush, Colonel," Lieutenant Thann Tyler said. "I don't like it."

The words were barely out of his mouth before a whooping, yapping line of mounted Shawnees thundered over the crest on the north side, guns popping and arrows flying. The troopers brought up their carbines and the officers whipped out their revolvers.

"Steady there, men!" Custer yelled. "There are more of us, and we can whip 'em!" He pulled his saber and nudged his horse to the forefront, shouting, "Cha-a-arge!"

Soldiers and Indians clashed in the middle of the meadow and battled it out for several minutes. Then the outnumbered Indians began to give way before the deadly fire of repeater rifles and six-shot revolvers. Their only recourse was hand-to-hand fighting.

Soon, many of the soldiers were off their mounts, with no time to reload, using the butts of empty rifles and revolvers as weapons. The sun winked off tomahawk blades and scalping knives as the fight continued.

Those soldiers still on their horses reloaded and fired intermittently when they could get a clear shot without hitting one of their own men.

Custer had sheathed his saber and was firing both .44s when a warrior yanked him off his horse, causing him to drop his guns. The Indian whipped a knife from its sheath and sprang at Custer, who was on his knees, trying to find his gun. Custer dodged and rolled, but the move threw him farther away from his weapons. Then he saw a scalping knife. Custer managed to avoid the warrior's blade and threw a stiff punch, cracking the Indian on the nose.

Thann Tyler was in hand-to-hand combat with a husky warrior wielding a tomahawk. Tyler held his empty revolver as the Indian came in for the kill. He dodged the blade and threw the gun at the Indian's face, clipping him slightly.

Thann surprised his opponent by dropping to the ground and rolling at his feet like a log. The Shawnee went down hard, and Thann was on him, striking the Indian's jaw with his fist. The blow stunned the Indian, and Thann grabbed his tomahawk and brought it down on the Indian's skull.

Thann gasped for breath and turned around to see the warriors dashing for their horses. Too many of their comrades had fallen, including their leader, and they were giving up the fight. What few were left made it to the horses and galloped away.

Tyler looked around for Custer, who stood over a Shawnee, a scalping knife protruding from the Indian's heart.

Captain Hays pointed his gun at a wounded Shawnee who stood watching his comrades ride away. He turned back to the captain and cried out for mercy in his native tongue. Every soldier watched as Hays dropped the hammer and the Indian went down.

Thann looked at Custer, expecting him to reprimand Hays, but Custer said only, "All right, men, let's pick up our dead and wounded and head back to the fort."

Thann's blood boiled all the way back to Fort Supply. He wanted to lash out at Hays for shooting down a man who was trying to surrender and at Custer for not chewing him out for doing it.

When they had been at Fort Supply for a full day, Tyler spoke to Custer at breakfast, asking him if they could have a private conversation.

The two officers took a stroll outside the fort. When they were out of earshot, Custer turned and said, "I know what this is about, Tyler, and I'm telling you right now to butt out."

"Colonel Custer, it's wrong—dead wrong—for a soldier to shoot a wounded, unarmed enemy who is surrendering."

"Maybe Captain Hays didn't understand that the man was wanting to surrender," Custer said.

Thann's mouth tightened. "You and I both know better. You should have read him out good and reported him for conduct unbecoming an officer of the United States Army."

Custer's face turned crimson and his smile looked wolfish as he said, "You're out of line, Lieutenant! Talk about conduct unbecoming an officer of the U.S. Army! Where does a lieutenant get the gall to tell a lieutenant colonel what he should do?"

"Comes from inside, Colonel," Thann said. "It got me right down in the pit of the stomach to see that Indian killed when he was surrendering. When you make excuses for it and won't do anything about it, I get the same feeling in my stomach all over again."

"Well, if you're so soft, why don't you get yourself transferred to another unit?"

"*That*, Mr. Custer," Thann said, "is exactly what I'm going to do!"

The next day, Lieutenant Thann Tyler left General Philip Sheridan's office and rode northeast to Fort Abraham Lincoln, where he had been assigned to General Alfred Terry's command.

CHAPTER
TWENTY

———— ◆ ————

In early November 1874, General Terry received a wire from Washington that he must dispatch a large unit of soldiers from Fort Abraham Lincoln to help army forces in western Nebraska, eastern Wyoming, and eastern Montana.

Under orders of his superiors, Lieutenant Colonel George Custer had led an expedition into the Black Hills of western Dakota Territory and the army had learned there was gold in the hills.

To the Sioux, the Black Hills territory held special religious significance. They were enraged at the intrusion into their sacred land. To make matters worse, word spread quickly about the gold, and a rush of white men descended on the hills with gold fever.

Custer had returned to Fort Lincoln to handle more Indian problems in that area. The white gold seekers had been driven from the Black Hills by the Sioux, but to retaliate for the intrusion, Red Cloud and Sitting Bull and their Cheyenne and Arapaho allies had accelerated their efforts to massacre white civilians in the areas farther west and to wipe out as many soldiers as possible.

General Terry sent Major Marcus Reno to Fort Laramie with four hundred men, Thann Tyler among them. They were to use the fort as a base to scout the area and put down any Indian uprising against the settlements.

Thann's parents were thrilled to see him and happy to hear of his promotion to captain. He shared with them how John Stranger had led him to Christ, imploring them to turn to the Lord. After several weeks of talking and spending time with them in the Scriptures, both parents opened their hearts to Jesus.

In January 1875, Thann led a company of men south of Fort Laramie to patrol the areas around the settlements. Since winter had set in, Indian attack on the settlements had lessened, and the army wanted to deter them further with the patrols.

Shaffer's Crossing, located at a wide place on the North Platte River, allowed wagons and riders on horseback to cross quite easily, even in midsummer. Point Laurel, a small settlement ten miles from Shaffer's Crossing, was named for the first family that settled there ten years previously. There were several farms and ranches close by.

Though the sun was shining, snow lay on the ground and the wind was raw. The soldiers rode with the collars of their tunics turned up and their hats pulled low.

They were welcomed at Shaffer's Crossing and invited into the homes of the settlement's few residents to get warm. No one had seen Indians on the plains since early December.

Then the patrol rode farther south toward Point Laurel. They were within six miles of the settlement when Lieutenant Alex Hancock, who rode next to Tyler, stood up in his stirrups. "Captain, there's somebody coming this way on foot. See him?"

A tiny dark dot on the snow seemed to stagger in their direction. "Something's wrong," Tyler said. "Let's go!"

Snow flew up behind galloping hooves as Tyler led his company across the windswept prairie.

"Captain, it's a woman!" Even as Hancock spoke, the woman fell. She struggled to get up and fell again.

Thann could see that the woman was quite young—barely

in her twenties. She wore a dark overcoat and her long blonde hair was streaming behind her in the wind. Tyler slid from his saddle and rushed to help her up.

"It's horrible! Just horrible!" she said, and started to go down again, but Thann steadied her with strong hands.

"What's horrible, ma'am?" he said.

She brushed the hair from her eyes and looked back in the direction she had come. "The Cheyennes. They...they attacked us at dawn this morning! Everybody's dead!"

"Are you talking about Point Laurel, ma'am?"

"Yes! Everybody's dead! They killed them all!" She drew a shuddering breath. "I hid from them. They didn't know I was there, or they would have killed me, too. Both of my parents and my brothers and sisters...and everybody else in the settlement! All one hundred and thirty-three of them are dead!"

Her body sagged against his chest. "Are you hurt?" Tyler asked, holding her up.

"I...I think my left ankle may be broken. I was hiding in the hayloft of Papa's barn. When the killing was over and the Cheyennes rode away, I was crying so hard and shaking so bad that I fell while climbing down the ladder. Everybody's dead, Captain!" she said, breaking into sobs. "I found all of them!"

"Ma'am, I'll send some of my men to check it out. If you've broken your ankle, we need to get you to the doctor at the fort. You can ride with me. May I lift you into the saddle?"

"Yes, please," she said, wiping her tears.

When Thann had placed her in the saddle, he said, "I haven't even told you my name, ma'am. I'm Captain Thann Tyler. We're from Fort Laramie. My father, Colonel Theron Tyler, is commandant."

She rubbed her cold hands together. "I'm Susan Laurel, Captain. It was my father, Dan Laurel, who established Point Laurel ten years ago."

"Yes, ma'am. I'm so sorry for what has happened."

Susan nodded, biting her lip.

Tyler told her he'd send half of his men to Point Laurel to look it over. He and the others would get her to the fort as quickly as possible.

Tyler instructed Lieutenant Hancock to stop at Shaffer's Crossing on the way back and tell the people what happened. As a safety precaution, they would stay with the residents until relieved by more soldiers from the fort. The obvious presence of the army in Shaffer's Crossing would keep the hostiles away.

Hancock's unit rode south, and Tyler led his men toward the fort. Susan sat in front of him, firmly held by his strong arms. While they rode, Susan told Thann about how her family had come west from Wisconsin a decade ago. Her parents wanted to begin a new life on the frontier. Things had gone well at Point Laurel until the Indians went on the warpath. Some people had packed up and gone back east.

Thann told Susan a little bit about his parents, then they rode in silence for several minutes. Thann could tell Susan was crying.

"Miss Susan, I wish I could ease the pain in your heart." He paused, then added, "But there is One who can."

Susan straightened and turned around as far as she could. "Lieutenant, are you speaking of the Lord in heaven?"

"I sure am, ma'am. The Lord Jesus Christ. A person must have Him living in his heart—"

"He does live in my heart," she said softly. "I've been a Christian since I was eight years old. My parents...my parents raised me in a home where the Bible was read and studied every day and prayer was a vital part of our lives. Jesus is my Saviour and my Friend. I love Him with all my heart."

When Thann and his patrol arrived at the fort with Susan Laurel, Dr. Randall Rogers went right to work on her ankle. Rogers discovered that her ankle was not broken, but it was badly sprained. She would have to use crutches for a couple of weeks.

The doctor was adjusting the crutches to fit Susan's small frame when the door opened and Thann came in with his parents. The colonel and Andrea Tyler sympathized with Susan in her grief and expressed their joy at learning she was a Christian.

Andrea sat down beside Susan and put an arm around her shoulder. "We have an extra bedroom in our quarters. You can make our home your home as long as you wish."

Susan wrapped her arms around Andrea's neck and wept.

The next day, Colonel Tyler sent a unit of soldiers to Shaffer's Crossing to relieve Lieutenant Hancock and his men. Hancock reported that every resident of Point Laurel, with the exception of Susan, had been killed. They had buried the bodies.

Thann and Susan spent a good deal of time together over the next two weeks. On the day Dr. Rogers was to examine her ankle to see if she could walk on her own, Thann commented on how well she was keeping up with him as they crossed the parade ground. "You've gotten pretty good with those things."

"Just when it's time to get rid of them," she said with a chuckle.

Thann stood near as the doctor examined Susan's foot and ankle. "Have you been putting a little weight on it from time to time as I suggested?"

"Yes, when I've moved around in my room."

"Well, I think you're ready to throw the crutches away and go back to normal. Put your shoe back on and let me see you stand up."

Susan laced up her shoe and rose to her feet. Gingerly she moved about, saying it felt quite tender, but she was sure if she took it easy, she could walk without the crutches.

Thann gave her his arm to walk her back to the colonel's quarters. They moved slowly, greeting soldiers along the way. Susan walked with a definite limp, but it felt good to be rid of the crutches.

When they reached his parents' quarters, Thann said, "Let's get you inside. You need to sit down and rest for awhile."

Thann pushed the door open to let Susan go first. Suddenly her ankle gave way, and Thann grabbed her to keep her from falling. "Maybe too far a walk for the first day," he said. "Let me help you."

He lifted her in his arms and carried her inside. He was about to lower her onto the couch when their eyes met and held. Their lips came together in a tender kiss, then Thann said, "I didn't get my face slapped, so I guess it was all right for me to kiss you."

She smiled and they kissed again.

Thann eased Susan onto the couch and dropped to one knee and took her hand. "Susan, I don't know how else to do this except to come right out and say it—I'm in love with you, lock, stock, and barrel."

"The Lord has been so good to me," she said. "The same day He took my parents home to heaven, He brought you into my life. I'm in love with you, too, darling. You're God's special gift to me."

The love between Thann Tyler and Susan Laurel grew deeper as the weeks passed. In early March, Thann proposed and they set the wedding date for Thann's birthday in June. Since Fort Laramie had no chaplain, the law allowed Theron Tyler, the fort's commandant, to perform the wedding. Andrea and Susan happily worked on Susan's wedding dress.

Thann was involved in a few skirmishes until the winter passed into spring, then there were some major battles as the

Indians renewed their attacks on white settlements, wagon trains, and stagecoaches.

When the wedding was less than a week away, the young couple was sitting on a bench outside Thann's quarters, enjoying the moonlight. Susan saw a look of sadness come into Thann's eyes. "What is it, darling? Something's bothering you."

He nodded. "I've been thinking about Quiet Thunder and Night Star. I wish they could attend the wedding."

"I guess that would be impossible."

"There's no way I could approach the Oglala village to invite them. Like Crazy Horse, most of the Indians are so full of hatred toward whites that they won't even honor a white flag anymore. And I don't know for sure if Quiet Thunder is still alive. But if he is, he has no idea I'm here at Fort Laramie. Only the Lord could bring us together again."

The wedding took place as scheduled on Thann's twenty-second birthday. There would be no honeymoon, for the hostiles were savagely attacking whites all over the territory, and Thann had to lead his own platoon against them.

On a hot day in late August, Colonel Tyler called Major Marcus Reno and Thann to his office. As they sat down in front of his desk, he said, "Gentlemen, I have orders from Washington. Some five hundred new troops are being sent here from Fort Lincoln to replace you and your men. General Terry has put in a request to have you back in Dakota Territory, and since the big brass in Washington esteems him highly, he gets what he wants."

"And that's it?" Reno said.

"You know the U.S. Army."

"So when does this happen?" Thann asked.

"The troops are on their way. They should arrive in about two weeks."

———

A few days later, Thann and his men were on a routine patrol northeast of Fort Laramie when they heard gunfire beyond a line of rolling hills. Thann put his troops to a gallop, and when they had topped a hill, they saw a circle of wagons and a band of Sioux warriors galloping away in the distance. Two warriors straggled behind the others. One was wounded and the other was lifting him back onto his horse.

There was something familiar about the one helping his comrade. Thann took binoculars from his saddlebag and focused them. Yes! It was Quiet Thunder!

Tyler turned to Lieutenant Hancock. "Lieutenant, there are a couple of hostiles out there who've been left behind. I know one of them. You see to the folks in the wagon train, and I'll be back shortly."

"Sir, you're not going to ride out there alone!"

"It's all right, believe me. You see to these people."

Tyler galloped toward his blood brother, waving his hat and shouting Quiet Thunder's name as he rode.

The blood brothers spoke quickly. Thann told Quiet Thunder about Susan and their wedding, and how he wished Quiet Thunder and Night Star could have been there.

"Quiet Thunder, my unit is being transferred back to Fort Lincoln. We have to leave in a few days. I've been afraid to approach your village with the way things are."

"I understand," Quiet Thunder said, nodding sadly.

"Could you bring Night Star and Blue Sky to the fort? Your mother, too?"

"I can do that, my brother. We will come tonight."

"Great! I'll alert the sentries that you're coming. When?"

"About two hours after darkness falls."

———

Quiet Thunder, his little family, and Gentle Fawn, appeared at the fort's gate as promised. Thann was there to greet them and took them back to his quarters where Susan, Andrea, and the Colonel waited.

Susan loved them instantly. She took Blue Sky in her arms and held her as they talked into the night.

When it was time for the Indians to leave, Thann opened his Bible and read a few passages about heaven. They might not have any more time together here, but they would have all eternity together in heaven.

Susan and Night Star developed a special closeness that night, though their time together had been brief. When Night Star embraced Susan in parting, she said, "I already love you, my sister. May our wonderful God keep you in His powerful hand."

"The bond we have in Jesus is such a precious thing, Night Star," Susan said. "We can pray for each other and stay close in our hearts."

When the Indians were on their horses and about to ride away, Quiet Thunder looked at Thann affectionately and spoke their familiar farewell, "Blood brothers forever."

"Blood brothers *forever*," Thann said.

On September 2, 1875, Major Reno led his troops east toward Fort Lincoln. Susan Tyler rode in the captain's personal wagon, joined periodically by other officers' wives. They arrived at the fort on September 28.

In late March 1876, two good things happened to Thann Tyler. On the twenty-seventh, he was promoted to major. On the thirtieth, Susan gave birth to a baby boy.

Fort Lincoln had a hospital with several rooms. When the baby was brought to Susan's room, Thann was standing by the bed, holding her hand. The nurse smiled and said, "Would you like to hold your little son, Major?" She handed him the little bundle and left the room.

Thann and Susan, with love and gratitude in their hearts, thanked the Lord for their healthy baby. Then Thann said, "Honey, it's time to give him his name."

"What do you want to name him?" she asked with a smile.

"Well...you know how much I love my blood brother."

"Of course."

"And the name has to start with *Th.*"

"Yes, Thann."

His words came out in a rush. "How do you like the sound of Thunder Tyler? Thunder—starts with *Th,* you see."

"Thunder, as in Quiet Thunder."

"Mm-hmm."

Susan chewed her lower lip. "Thunder Tyler. You're sure?"

"You don't like it," he said, disappointment in his voice.

"Well, it...ah...it's different."

"Well, so's *Thann.* You never heard that name before, did you?"

Susan reached up and said, "May I hold Thunder Tyler now?"

Thann's face beamed as he handed her the baby. "Susan Marie Tyler, you're the most wonderful mother on earth!"

"Well, I ought to be," she said with a giggle. "What other mother in the world can say she gave birth to Thunder?"

Chiefs Red Cloud, Sitting Bull, Two Suns, and Bear Killer were in Sitting Bull's village, along with their sub-chiefs, discussing the continued white invasion of soldiers and settlers. By mutual agreement they would ally themselves for all-out war.

Soon small army forts in Wyoming and Montana Territories were reporting to Washington that the hostiles were assembling in massive numbers.

On April 28, 1876, General Alfred Terry received orders from Washington to take the entire Seventh Cavalry Regiment and head west. He must begin military preparations in the vicinity of the headwaters of the Powder, Tongue, Rosebud, and Big Horn Rivers. The big brass in Washington had decided that the biggest sources of trouble would come from Sitting Bull, Gall, Red Cloud, and the Oglala sub-chief called Crazy Horse.

The edict from Washington was clear—bring those tribes into subjection or annihilate them.

TWENTY-ONE

Fort Abraham Lincoln was a beehive of activity for the next eighteen days as the Seventh Cavalry Regiment prepared for the westward expedition.

On May 16, 1876, Brigadier General Terry sent his adjutant, Lieutenant Clyde Harrison, to spread the word that he would meet with all his officers at 2:00 P.M. sharp.

Just before 2:00, the officers quickly assembled at the tent flying the red and blue pennant with white crossed sabers that marked the Seventh's regimental headquarters. Several other U.S. Army regiments were stationed at Fort Lincoln and had their own regimental headquarters.

General Terry, a tall, thin man with salt-and-pepper hair, beard, and mustache, called the meeting to order. Behind him stood a tripod holding a large map of the region they were headed to.

The plans were complete and contacts had been made with military leaders already in the west. The Seventh would ride out of Fort Lincoln the next day. Other forces would join the 694 men when they reached the south end of the Little Bighorn Valley in southern Montana Territory.

General George A. Crook was bringing 1,000 men from Fort Fetterman, Wyoming, and Colonel John Gibbon was heading a combined group of 450 infantrymen and cavalrymen from Fort Shaw and Fort Ellis, both in Montana.

Terry would plan his moves once they had rendezvoused with Crook and Gibbon on the Rosebud River at the southern-most tip of the Little Big Horn Valley.

That evening, Susan Tyler prepared a special meal for her husband. After supper, they sat in the parlor of their quarters and took turns holding little Thunder. When the baby had been put to bed, they stepped onto the porch.

As they looked up at the half-moon and the shimmering stars, Susan's voice broke. "Thunder and I will miss you so much, darling."

Thann cupped her face in his hands and brushed the tears from her cheeks. "I love you, Mrs. Tyler." They kissed, then held each other for a long time.

The sun was beginning its morning arc as the Seventh U.S. Cavalry Regiment began forming into prearranged lines. General Terry stood looking on with his wife as the officers' horses were brought to the parade ground by troopers.

Susan was standing next to Thann, holding little Thunder as Lieutenant Colonel Custer walked by with his wife, Libbie, holding the crook of his arm. Custer was dressed in buckskins and wore a broad-brimmed white hat and the usual red scarf around his neck.

"Thann," Susan said, "what happened to Custer's long curls?"

Thann chuckled. "He got a haircut yesterday. Somebody said he did it because the Sioux hate him with a passion and will be looking for him when they get into battle. They won't be able to identify him as easily without a uniform and without his long hair."

At that instant, Custer's eyes happened to settle on Thann. The lieutenant colonel quickly looked the other way.

"He just plain doesn't like you, honey."

"What was your first clue?" Thann said. "For that matter, the man hasn't spoken one word to me since we came back to Fort Lincoln. I'm just glad I don't have to fight under him. Major Reno and I get along fine."

The army band was assembling near the gate, their brass instruments glistening in the sun. The call came for the officers to mount up. Thann kissed Susan and held her close with the baby between them.

"Thann, I wish you didn't have to go."

"It's what soldiers do, sweetheart," he said softly. "I'll be back in a few weeks or so. I love you."

Thann pulled back the corner of the blanket from his little son's face. "Thunder, you take care of Mommy while Daddy's away."

As he bent to kiss the baby's forehead, Susan began to weep.

All the officers swung into their saddles first. Included were Brigadier General Alfred Terry, Lieutenant Colonel George Custer, Major Marcus Reno, Major Thann Tyler, Captain Frederick Benteen, Captain Miles Keogh, and Captain Thomas Custer, who would ride next to his older brother.

Once the men were in their saddles, they were to look straight ahead as the column moved out.

The band played "The Girl I Left Behind Me," as Susan Tyler stood with the other wives and children waving to the soldiers' backs. She offered up a silent prayer as she watched Thann until he passed from view.

On June 21, General Terry and his long column of fighting men arrived at the south end of the Little Bighorn Valley, some twenty-five miles east of the Little Bighorn River.

Colonel Gibbon and his 450 men had arrived a day and a half earlier.

General Crook and his 1,000 men were not there. General Terry and Colonel Gibbon were unaware that on June 17, Crook's column had been attacked by 1,000 Sioux and Cheyenne warriors at the Rosebud River, sixty miles northeast of the rendezvous point. The leader of the Indian attack was the Oglala sub-chief, Crazy Horse.

While they waited for Crook's men, General Terry ordered Major Reno to take a small detachment on a scouting trip to see if they could find any sign of a large force of Indians.

Reno chose twelve men. The only officer was Major Thann Tyler.

At the close of the day, Reno and Tyler returned to report they had found an Indian trail headed toward the Little Bighorn River, also called the Greasy Grass by the Sioux, which was the eastern tributary of the Bighorn River. Apparently the Indians had moved a camp from the east, from one spot to another, several times. Reno had not seen them by the time he had to turn around and head back.

General Terry could wait no longer for General Crook. He needed to strike while the iron was hot. He sat down with the officers and outlined a plan, drawing a map in the dirt. The Indians were probably camped by now somewhere north on the Little Bighorn. The Seventh Cavalry and Colonel Gibbon's troops would catch up to them, launch an attack, and wipe them out.

General Terry explained that the Seventh would divide into three units. Custer's unit would consist of 231 men. Reno would command 112. The other 351 would go with Gibbon and his troops.

Terry would send Custer and Reno up a small creek to a point where they would turn and cross the Wolf Mountains. Then they would move onto the Little Bighorn from the south.

From there, they would ride the banks of the Little Bighorn north.

Terry would go with Colonel Gibbon and move north along the Bighorn River at a parallel with Custer and Reno. This would keep them an average of ten miles apart, which would make it impossible for Sioux scouts working along the Little Bighorn to spot Gibbon's larger army. Terry had beefed up the Gibbon unit because it would be the one to surprise the Indians by entering the Little Bighorn Valley from the north. The Sioux would then be crushed between the two forces.

By firelight, as the Seventh and Gibbon's forces camped for the night, General Terry sat down with Colonel Gibbon, Lieutenant Colonel Custer, and Majors Reno and Tyler.

Terry directed his remarks to Custer, while the others listened. "I want you to keep your march down to thirty miles a day, Colonel Custer. Colonel Gibbon and I will do the same. You've had a flare for marching your men too hard, and I want it understood that you're to hold it down. This is a much higher altitude than Kansas, and you'll wear your men out if you push them harder. Is that understood?"

Sparks had flown between Terry and Custer on several occasions in the past. Now Terry was putting the bit in Custer's mouth, and it rankled him.

Terry had drawn another map in the dust with a broken tree limb. "Tomorrow is Thursday, gentlemen. By marching thirty miles a day, Colonel Custer, you will be just about…here by Sunday." He was pointing to a spot along a wavy line that represented the Little Bighorn. "Do you follow?"

"Yes, sir."

"It will take another day's march for Colonel Gibbon and me, coming from the opposite direction, to meet up with you. Those Indians are bound to be somewhere in the area where you will stop on Sunday. Between your scouts and ours, we'll have them spotted. We'll meet you on Monday the twenty-sixth, and launch an attack on the Sioux camp the same day. Understand?"

"Yes, sir." Custer lifted his broad-brimmed white hat and ran his fingers through his hair.

Terry continued. "Sitting Bull and Red Cloud will have a large force. We know that. Let's not anybody try to take them on without the joint effort of both our columns. Hopefully, General Crook and his thousand will find us before we engage in the fight."

As he stood up and the others followed suit, General Terry's attention turned to Custer once again. "Colonel Custer, I want to press this point home. If your scouts spot the Sioux camp before Colonel Gibbon and I show up, hide yourselves and send a runner to us so we'll know you've found them. We'll do the same for you. Do not—I repeat, do *not* try to whip them all by yourself. Stay on the parallel of thirty miles a day as I've commanded. Position yourselves on Sunday in the general area I have designated, and wait for us to meet you. I want us to fight them together.

"When the battle is joined, you can rest assured that Sitting Bull, Gall, Red Cloud, and Crazy Horse will bring the full pressure of their strength upon us. I want to match that strength and more with every man and gun we have. Understand?"

Custer's face went crimson. "The Seventh can lick any Sioux army those redskins can put against us! No offense to your troops, Colonel Gibbon."

Gibbon dipped his chin in a sober nod but did not reply.

Custer looked back at Terry. "I'll do as you say, sir. Thirty miles a day. We won't get ahead of you and Colonel Gibbon's troops." With that, Custer snapped a salute and stomped off into the darkness.

At two hours before dawn, Terry and Gibbon rode out ahead of the 450 infantrymen and cavalrymen, angling northwest toward the Bighorn River. Terry needed to get a head start on their longer journey, so they pulled out while the Seventh Cavalry still slept.

At the crack of dawn, the men of the Seventh rose from their bedrolls and ate a cold breakfast of beef jerky, hardtack, and water. Custer's four scouts rode out immediately, eating their breakfast as they rode.

Thirty minutes after sunrise, the column was almost ready to go.

Marcus Reno and Thann Tyler were cinching up their McClellan saddles, along with the rest of the officers, when Custer approached. He gave Tyler a glance, then said, "Major Reno, your column will ride up the left bank of the creek, and mine will ride on the right. Better to have firepower on both sides, since we don't know when the hostiles might come at us."

"Yes, sir," Reno said.

Custer swung into his saddle and gave his Seventh Cavalry the once-over. The 350-mile jaunt from Fort Lincoln had toughened them. The summer sun had tanned their faces the color of mahogany. Their uniforms were wrinkled, having been slept in for over a month, and rain had faded and stained their shirts and hats.

Custer pushed his horse to the front, took his position beside his brother Tom, and gave the signal to move out. When they reached the creek, Major Reno and his men splashed across and rode the left bank.

As the day progressed and the sun heated up the land, there was little conversation among the troops, though every man kept his eyes peeled for any sign of Indians. Horses snorted and blew while their tails swished at flies. By midmorning the men were drinking from their canteens often and sleeving away sweat. They had covered their thirty miles by an hour before sunset. Custer was tempted to push on till dark, but decided to let his men rest.

Friday was just as hot and uneventful, and so was Saturday. From what Custer could tell, they were somewhat ahead of schedule, but he didn't let it worry him. They would ride a little slower tomorrow.

On Sunday morning, Thann Tyler and a few others gathered in a shady spot under some cottonwoods and sang hymns during the few minutes of free time allotted to all the men. Thann was the unofficial chaplain of the group. After he read Scripture, one of the sergeants who had known him for a couple of years spoke up. "Hey, guys. You know what today is?"

"Sunday," someone said.

"June 25, 1876," came another reply.

"Well, it's also Major Tyler's twenty-third birthday!" the sergeant said.

While the men wished Thann a happy birthday, George Custer shouted that it was almost time to pull out.

Within two hours, the Seventh Cavalry reached the Little Bighorn River and headed north. They soon found evidence of an Indian camp that had been there in the last few days.

Custer halted the column and told the men to dismount for a ten-minute break. He and his brother moved across the ground where the Sioux had camped. Major Reno drew up. "Colonel," he said, "by the looks of the horse droppings, I'd say they were here day before yesterday. Probably pulled out early yesterday morning."

"That's the way it looks to me, Major," Custer said. "Looks like maybe their scouts have spotted us, and we've got them on the run."

"Could be."

Tom Custer scanned the area and said, "How many you think are in the camp, Armstrong?"

"Hard to tell. Five or six hundred, maybe. But they're not all warriors. By the footprints I see here, there are plenty of women and children. Probably not more than a couple hundred warriors."

When the column resumed their northward move, George Custer was exhilarated. It felt good to know he had the stubborn savages on the run. He hipped around in the saddle and commanded the column to put their horses to a trot.

Some fifteen miles north of the trotting cavalrymen, the Sioux, Cheyenne, and Arapaho had set up an encampment on the west bank of the Little Bighorn River at the base of a long, grassy slope to the east that extended almost a mile to its crest. Sitting Bull's Hunkpapas and Red Cloud's Oglalas had already been there for a week. Two Suns' Arapahos had arrived two days previously, and Bear Killer's Cheyennes had arrived the day before, one unit having come from the east and another from the south. It was the southern unit of Cheyennes whose camp Custer had found.

Fifteen thousand Indians were camped amidst a dense stand of elms, willows, and cottonwoods that lined the river on both sides and spread out to the west. There were four thousand warriors, most armed with repeater rifles they had stolen from dead soldiers and from army supply wagon trains. The rest were women, children, and old men.

Chief Red Cloud was not with them. He had taken two hundred warriors several miles to the north to attack an army wagon train delivering arms and supplies to forts in northern Montana Territory. Crazy Horse had been left in charge of the Oglala warriors.

The Sioux scouts had spotted Custer's and Reno's troops on the move north the day before, and Sitting Bull was preparing to greet them. He explained to his sub-chiefs that he would direct the battle from a distant hill. Crazy Horse would be the one to actually lead the warriors in the attack. Two Suns and Bear Killer agreed that the great force of Indians should have one leader and that it should be Crazy Horse. Though Gall was older and had been a sub-chief much longer than Crazy Horse, he knew the young warrior sub-chief was a better leader.

All the sub-chiefs were briefed, then Crazy Horse called Quiet Thunder aside and told him to take two warriors and ride south. They were to make sure the soldier coats were still headed toward the Indian camp.

Quiet Thunder embraced Night Star, who was in the camp with thousands of other squaws, and explained that he must ride on a scouting mission. He kissed little Blue Sky, then turned his attention to the tiny baby boy in his crib outside their teepee, shaded by a tall willow tree.

Night Star moved up beside her husband. She was very pleased that the Lord had allowed her to give Quiet Thunder a son. The proud father tenderly stroked the baby's cheek.

Quiet Thunder and his companions rode south for about an hour before they saw the column of soldiers still heading up the west bank of the Little Bighorn. The sight of the dark-blue uniforms made Quiet Thunder's thoughts run to his blood brother. He was glad Thann was back east at Fort Abraham Lincoln.

The Oglala scouts wheeled their mounts and galloped back to camp. Quiet Thunder reported to Sitting Bull and the sub-chiefs that the soldier coats were moving north at a trot. He estimated they would reach the Indian camp within two hours.

Custer's scouts had dashed back to inform the lieutenant colonel that they had spotted a handful of Sioux warriors on the west bank of the Little Bighorn about two miles ahead. Beyond them, about three miles, was an Indian encampment, but they couldn't tell how large it was for the trees.

The scouts' report caused George Custer to sit up in the saddle, his eyes flashing like polished silver.

"Good work, gentlemen!" he said.

The column had halted when the scouts arrived. Now Custer twisted around in his saddle and ordered, "Major Reno, take your men and kill the handful of Indians down there on the riverbank."

Thann Tyler was closer to Custer than Reno and decided to speak. "Pardon me, Colonel, but that handful of Indians might very well be a setup. I suggest that both units go down there."

"I don't recall speaking to you, Major Tyler. I was speaking to Major Reno, who is the commander of your unit."

Reno nudged his horse closer, saying, "Major Tyler could be right, sir. It might be a trap. It would be safer if—"

"Major Reno, is my judgment being questioned! Do as I say. If it turns out to be a trap, we'll reinforce you in a hurry. Now, move out!"

As Reno's unit dropped over the edge of a ridge to converge on the small group of Indians, Custer said to his brother, "There's no way that situation down there could be a trap. We've just caught those thick-headed savages off guard."

When Tom didn't comment, Custer said, "We know from the campsite back there that there are only a couple hundred warriors up ahead. There are 231 of us, and we've got better weapons. While Reno's taking care of those few warriors, we'll ride ahead and wipe out the camp."

When Major Reno and his men drew near the small group of Indians, a swarm of warriors came out of the brush, firing their rifles. The soldiers were forced to dismount and take refuge in a large stand of trees.

As the battle grew fierce, Reno kept looking for Custer to come over the ridge as he had promised. Finally, Reno called to a lieutenant, telling him to ride out and tell Custer they were under attack.

Fear twisted the lieutenant's features. "Major, sir, there's no way I could make it to the horses now. The Indians will get me before I take a dozen steps."

"We'll cover you!" Reno said, angry at the lieutenant's hesitancy to obey an order. "Our lives depend on getting Custer's unit here to help us!"

Thann Tyler was firing his revolver a few feet away. Over his shoulder, he said, "Major Reno, I'll go find Custer! Cover me!"

Custer led his men off the slopes toward what appeared to be a sleepy Indian camp on a hot summer day. The tall, dense stand of trees along the riverbank spread out to the meadows westward and concealed the better part of the encampment.

Custer's eyes lit up with glee. "Look, Tom! We've caught them napping!"

He called for the column to halt and turned his horse to face his men. "All right, gentlemen, we're going to put ourselves in the history books today! This will be the beginning of the end for the whole Lakota nation!"

Suddenly the group heard galloping hooves as Major Tyler came over a rise behind them and skidded his mount to a halt. "Colonel, we're under attack back there! It was a trap, just as Major Reno and I feared!"

Custer glanced toward the Indian camp on the riverbank. "Reno will have to wait, Tyler," he said. "Right now we're in a position to wipe out that camp down there, and we're going to do it!"

"But, sir, General Terry told you to sit tight and wait for him and Colonel Gibbon! They won't be here till tomorrow!"

"Tomorrow may be too late," Custer said. "We've got to hit them now! That's final, Major Tyler!"

Custer left Tyler sitting on his horse and led his men toward the Indian camp. Tyler wheeled his horse, intending to return to Major Reno, then hauled up short. His blood turned to ice as he saw a swarm of warriors thunder toward him on horseback. He could tell by their war paint and headdresses that they were Cheyenne.

His only hope now was to join Custer and his men.

CHAPTER
TWENTY-TWO

❖

Custer and his men were within three hundred yards of the Indian encampment when Custer realized he'd led his men into a trap. Countless warriors came swarming at them out of the trees and over a low hill. More than half of them were on foot, holding repeater rifles.

The soldiers were waiting for Custer's orders when they saw Major Tyler galloping up from the rear, a wave of mounted Indians on his tail. As Tyler drew up, Custer pointed to the long grassy slope to the east. "Over there, men! If we can reach the crest, we'll have the advantage of high ground!"

Custer put his horse to a gallop and his men followed. The sounds of gunfire crackled behind them. They soon found there were deep gullies and ditches they hadn't seen from the lower elevation. It took extra time to thread their way around the deep spots, but before long they were riding hard for higher ground.

Custer's heart froze as a phalanx of mounted Sioux, Cheyenne, and Arapaho came over the east ridge. They spread out in a fan shape to close in the soldiers on three sides. Custer looked back toward the river and saw hundreds of Indians coming on foot where the ditches and gullies pocked the hillside. Custer shouted for his men to dismount, shoot their horses, and use their bodies as shields.

Thann's stomach went sour as he slid from his saddle, put his revolver to his horse's head, and squeezed the trigger. He went down on his belly behind the horse's body, blasting away. There was no need to aim. The waves of Indians were so thick there was no way to miss.

Scalplocks fluttered from the barrel tips of stolen army rifles and war whoops dinned toward the men, who were scattered for a hundred yards down the slope to the west.

The mounted Indians began to slide from their horses and charge on foot. The air turned thick with smoke as the Indians ripped into Custer's ranks with U.S. army-issue rifles. The men of the Seventh fought back gallantly.

Crazy Horse was off his mount near the top of the hill when he saw a young trooper crawling toward him. The trooper's pant-leg was shiny with crimson. He had dropped his rifle and was trying to get out of the line of fire.

Crazy Horse shouldered his repeater rifle and shouted, "Hokahey, soldier coat! It is a good day to die!" then fired.

Custer raised his head above the body of his horse and stared about at his doomed men. He shouted hoarse words of encouragement to them.

What had begun as another quiet morning was now a deafening cacophony of whooping warriors, shouting soldiers, and gunfire. After using all their ammunition, paint-daubed Indians hurled themselves at the soldiers, wielding knives and tomahawks. Bullets crisscrossed the hot summer air, buzzing like angry hornets. The entire hillside was enveloped in thick clouds of dust and smoke.

Thann Tyler could see they were outnumbered at least twenty to one. His mind flashed back to John Stranger, who had led him to Jesus. While he ducked his head to reload, he whispered, "Thank You, Lord, for saving me. Thank You for John Stranger, who pressed the gospel home to my heart."

As he opened fire again, Thann's mind raced to his precious

wife and son. He yearned for them, but he knew he'd see them again one day—in heaven.

When Thann ran out of cartridges for his revolver, he crawled to the dead horse next to his and picked up the fallen sergeant's carbine. He checked the magazine and found it full, then located more cartridges in the dead man's saddlebag and returned to his own spot.

Dead and dying cavalrymen dotted the hillside beneath a heavy cloud of smoke and dust. Off to Tyler's right, the cloud broke momentarily, and his attention was drawn to Tom Custer kneeling over the body of his older brother.

George Armstrong Custer was dead.

Suddenly Tom's body took several bullets and he fell dead on top of his brother.

Thann fired, taking out an Arapaho coming straight at him with a tomahawk. The Indian was dead before he hit the ground, but his momentum carried him all the way to Thann's horse and over. Thann rolled the corpse off him and fired at another Indian coming at him with a knife.

The din of battle was lessening. Thann knew it was because nearly half the Seventh Cavalry had been annihilated.

He shouldered the fully loaded rifle and fired at a shadowy figure in the smoke, and another Indian went down. Somewhere in the cloud that hung over the hillside, the loud voice of a red man called to another.

Thann jacked a cartridge into the chamber and swung his head in the direction of the shout. He thought he saw three Indians coming at him at the same time, but the dust and smoke was so thick it was hard to tell. If they were, this was his moment to die.

Thann rose to his knees and held the rifle ready, waiting for a clear target. Suddenly a gust of hot wind cleared a narrow swath before him. What he saw stabbed at his heart.

He had been ready to shoot his blood brother, and Quiet

Thunder's rifle was trained on his chest!

Time seemed to stand still. The clamor of the battle was gone.

While Thann was remembering the last words he and Quiet Thunder had spoken to each other, Crazy Horse's biting words were echoing in Quiet Thunder's mind: *If my nephew came face to face with his blood brother on the battlefield...*

Quiet Thunder's eyes filled with tears, as did Thann's, and both men lowered their rifles.

Before they could speak, Crazy Horse materialized out of the smoke, his carbine lined on Thann's chest. He quickly analyzed the situation and squeezed the trigger.

Quiet Thunder stood rooted to the spot, looking down at Thann.

Crazy Horse turned back to the battle and called over his shoulder, "I knew you could not do it!"

Quiet Thunder finally moved to sit on the ground and lift Thann's head and shoulders into his lap. Tears coursed through the dust and dirt on his cheeks as he clenched his teeth in agony of soul.

Thann's breath was bubbling in his lungs as he looked up and strained to focus on Quiet Thunder's face. He said, "Blood brothers...forever," then his body went limp and the bubbling ceased.

Quiet Thunder hugged Thann's body and rocked back and forth. "Yes, Thann! Blood brothers forever!"

As the battle played itself out, Quiet Thunder sat on the ground, holding Thann's lifeless body.

It took only another ten minutes for the massive force of Indians to bring about the last shot. The men of the Seventh Cavalry lay sprawled all over the hillside amid dead horses and the bodies of Sioux, Cheyenne, and Arapaho warriors. Quiet Thunder's attention was drawn from his dead blood brother momentarily when he heard some of the Indians shouting to each other that Yellow Hair was dead.

As was their custom, the Indians began mutilating the bodies to complete their victory. Heartsick and full of grief, Quiet Thunder carefully laid Thann down and rose to his feet. He walked away a few steps and surveyed the surrounding hills. He would pick a quiet, shady place to bury Thann.

A sudden rustling made him turn around. Two Arapaho warriors were ready to mutilate Thann's body.

"No!" he shouted in their language. "Do not touch that dead soldier coat!"

"We cut up all soldier coats except Yellow Hair! We do not want to dirty our hands on him!"

Quiet Thunder pointed a stiff finger and said, "You do not touch this one!"

The Arapaho's eyes bulged. "What is it, Oglala? You love the white eyes? You traitor?"

Blind fury sent Quiet Thunder after him. Before the Arapaho could so much as flinch, a rock-hard fist slammed his jaw, knocking him off his feet and sending him rolling down the slope. The other Indian gave Quiet Thunder a fearsome glance and went to see about his comrade.

Quiet Thunder stood over Thann Tyler's body and began to weep. He bent down and picked him up, cradling him in his arms, and whispered, "I promise no one will harm your body, my brother. I will take you down by the river in the shade of the trees and bury you with honor."

As he turned and headed toward the river, he noted that the encampment was gone. He knew what had happened. During the battle, Sitting Bull had sent orders for the women, children, and old men to move out. It would not take long for other army units to learn of the battle. He wanted to get the camp safely away.

Quiet Thunder looked toward the hill where Sitting Bull had been during the battle. Though he could not make out the warrior with Sitting Bull, he recognized Crazy Horse's pinto.

He began walking again, weaving among the bodies. The mutilation was still in progress. Quiet Thunder recognized two Hunkpapa warriors, Angry Dog and Hawk Eye, cutting up a soldier's body just a few feet away. But he was unaware of a young lieutenant who lay face-down a few yards ahead of him.

Lieutenant Louis Griffin was bleeding profusely from two bullet wounds and knew he was going to die. The Indians were mutilating bodies all around him. Soon they would get to him. He had two bullets left in his revolver. He would use one bullet on the first Indian who came near him and the second one on himself.

He lay very still as Quiet Thunder moved past him, carrying Thann Tyler's body. When Quiet Thunder was a dozen feet farther down the slope, Griffin cocked the hammer, aimed the barrel at Quiet Thunder's back, and fired.

Crazy Horse and Sitting Bull had left the hill and now rode toward the bloody slope. Many of the Indians were picking up the bodies of their dead comrades and laying them in a long line. Angry Dog and Hawk Eye had spotted the two Sioux leaders and ran toward them, waving for their attention.

"Crazy Horse!" Hawk Eye gasped. "We have bad news to tell you!"

Angry Dog let Hawk Eye tell the news that a soldier pretending to be dead had killed Quiet Thunder. When Quiet Thunder went down, the soldier coat put the gun to his own head and killed himself.

Crazy Horse's face remained impassive. He and Sitting Bull were on their way to the women, children, and old men who were moving southwest by Sitting Bull's orders. They wanted to make sure the women camped in a spot where the warriors could fight off the soldier coats if they had to.

Crazy Horse's mouth was a thin line as he said to Angry Dog and Hawk Eye, "You will make sure Quiet Thunder is buried honorably with the other Sioux warriors after seven days. We will tell his squaw of his death, as we will tell all squaws of husbands who were killed today. Because of this battle, soldier coats all over this territory will be very angry. Maybe come in great numbers. Squaws will not come to burial."

"We will see that Quiet Thunder is properly buried," Angry Dog said.

At sunset on Wednesday, June 28, a column of soldiers on horseback and riding in army supply wagons moved slowly eastward toward the Rosebud River. Major Reno and what was left of his battered and bedraggled unit were traveling back to Fort Abraham Lincoln with General Terry and the men of the Seventh Cavalry he had taken with Colonel Gibbon's troops up the Bighorn River. Gibbon and his men had headed back for Forts Shaw and Ellis.

Reno's wounded men were riding in the wagons, which the Seventh had brought with them from Fort Lincoln.

On Monday, after seeing the carnage at the Little Bighorn River, the men of Gibbon's unit and the men of the Seventh Cavalry were completely demoralized. General Terry, who had the authority to return them to Fort Lincoln, knew it would be months before they would be ready to fight again.

Terry had asked Colonel Gibbon to wire Washington, since he would arrive at Fort Shaw in less than a day's ride, and Washington would in turn wire Fort Lincoln with the tragic news of the battle.

Major Reno could only conjecture that Thann Tyler had

either been killed while riding to get Custer's help or had been caught up in the Little Bighorn battle. If he was still alive, he would have shown up by now. Reno shared his thoughts about Tyler with General Terry.

As shadows lengthened, the column drew up to the west bank of the Rosebud. They would camp there for the night and pull out at sunrise in the morning.

A sergeant happened to look back toward the sunset and saw two riders approaching. He brought them to General Terry's attention, and many of the men watched as the riders drew nearer.

Soon they could tell that the horses were pintos, and a few minutes later that the riders were Indian women. As they drew up, the soldiers saw that each woman was carrying a baby in a cradle board on her back. General Terry and Major Reno took a few steps to meet them as the men looked on.

"Good evening, ladies," Terry said. "Do you speak English?"

"Yes, we do," the younger one said. "I am Night Star of the Oglalas, and this is Gentle Fawn, mother of my husband who… who was killed in the battle on Sunday at the Little Bighorn River. The papooses are my son and daughter."

"I am sorry for the pain you feel, ma'am," Terry said. "Is there something I can do for you?"

"We have been traveling since early Monday morning," Night Star said. "We saw that you have wagons, and that you are heading east. I know we are considered your enemies, but since we are women and we have these papooses, we ask if we may travel with you and possibly ride in one of your wagons. The papooses… they grow tired of being tied in the cradle boards."

"Ma'am, we do not consider Indian women and children our enemies. You are welcome to ride in our wagons. How far east are you going?"

"Fort Abraham Lincoln."

The general and the major looked at each other in surprise.

"Well, ma'am," Terry said, "that is exactly where we're going."

Night Star and Gentle Fawn exchanged glances and smiles.

"Pardon me, ladies," Reno said, "but why would you be going to Fort Lincoln?"

"We must pay a visit to Susan Tyler."

"You are friends of Mrs. Tyler? The wife of Major Thann Tyler?"

"Yes. As I am sure you know, Major Tyler was killed in the battle on Sunday."

"Well, ma'am," Terry said, "we really weren't sure what happened to the major. It's a long story, but he was not a member of the unit that fought in the battle. He was sent on an errand to speak to the leader of that unit, and never returned. We could only assume that he was killed."

Night Star explained that her husband and Thann Tyler had been friends since they were very small and had become blood brothers. Oglala warriors had told her and Gentle Fawn of seeing Major Tyler killed in the battle. Quiet Thunder was carrying the major's body toward the river for burial when a young army officer, presumed dead, shot him in the back.

General Terry and his men were touched by the determination of these women to make a 350-mile trek because they wanted to be with Susan Tyler in her grief.

The two women and children were given a wagon to ride in with their horses tied behind.

The news of the massacre of Lieutenant Colonel George Custer and his men at the Little Bighorn reached Fort Abraham Lincoln by wire from Washington on Tuesday, June 27.

There was also word in the same wire that General Terry and Major Reno and their remaining men were returning to Fort

Lincoln. The message made it clear that Major Reno had lost the bulk of his men in a separate battle on the same day.

Susan Tyler knew that her husband would not have been fighting with Custer. Since some of Major Reno's men had survived their battle, she hoped and prayed that Thann might be alive.

On July 24, General Terry and his men crossed the border into Dakota Territory and were three days out of Fort Lincoln when they stopped to make camp beside a small stream.

As the sun was setting, Night Star and Gentle Fawn were washing clothes in the stream for the wounded men, whom they had cared for during the journey. The two women often spoke together of Quiet Thunder and Thann Tyler now walking together with Jesus and the Sky People in heaven. They were wringing water from shirts when they heard a shout.

"General Terry! Rider coming in from the west!"

All eyes turned toward the lone rider who came at a gallop, whipping up dust clouds.

The women moved to the center of camp and hung the wet clothes on the wagons to dry, then turned back to watch the rider. The orange glare of the setting sun made it hard to see the rider clearly, but they could see he was on a pinto.

"Looks like an Indian, General," Reno said.

Suddenly Gentle Fawn gasped. "Night Star! It is—"

"Quiet Thunder!" Night Star said. "He is alive! Oh, thank You, dear God! Quiet Thunder is alive!"

Terry, Reno, and the men moved in close to the women as both began to weep for joy.

As Quiet Thunder reined in, drawing the horse to a halt, Night Star ran to him, weeping and saying over and over again, "Oh, Quiet Thunder, we thought you were dead!"

Gentle Fawn waited her turn with tears streaming down her cheeks.

Quiet Thunder held Night Star for a long time as she wept against his shoulder. He was blinking back his own tears when he looked at his mother and motioned for her to come to him.

When everyone had settled down, Quiet Thunder asked to see his children. He held both of them on his lap by the fire as he and Night Star and Gentle Fawn began to piece together their stories.

"I will explain why I am alive in a moment," Quiet Thunder said. "First, tell me what you were told."

Night Star and Gentle Fawn told him what they knew, then added that none of the women had been allowed to go to the burials, by order of Sitting Bull and Crazy Horse.

Quiet Thunder explained that he was carrying Thann's body toward the river, where he planned to bury him with honor, when the army officer shot at him. The bullet grazed his head, knocking him unconscious.

He remained unconscious until the warriors found him breathing and took him to the river and revived him. They were going to take him on to the new campsite the night of the battle, but Quiet Thunder insisted he wanted to bury his blood brother the next morning.

After Thann was buried, the warriors who had stayed the night with Quiet Thunder helped him onto his horse, for he was having dizzy spells. By the time they arrived at the camp, the Oglala women told him that Night Star and Gentle Fawn had left for Fort Lincoln to see Susan Tyler, carrying the papooses.

Quiet Thunder had severe dizzy spells for several days, but as soon as he was able to ride, he left the camp to join his family. He tracked them to the spot where they had caught up to the army column and soon figured out they were traveling with the column.

Now that he had found them, he was glad to know that General Terry and his men were headed for Fort Lincoln.

CHAPTER
TWENTY-THREE

O n the morning of July 27, Susan Tyler fed little Thunder and laid him in his crib with a handmade rattle to play with, then knelt beside her bed to pray. She knew General Terry and Major Reno would arrive at the fort soon, and she would finally learn if Thann was alive. After spending nearly an hour in prayer, Susan sat down with her Bible and let the Lord speak to her heart as she read.

It was now late afternoon and Susan and an officer's wife from another regiment were sewing together at the kitchen table. Amy Cowen was a Christian too, and she and Susan spent a lot of time together. As yet the Cowens had no children, so Amy often took care of Thunder when Susan went to the commissary to shop.

When excited voices on the parade ground shouted that General Terry had arrived, Susan dropped her needle and thread and leaped to her feet.

"Oh, Amy, it's time."

"Do you want to wake Thunder? Or would you rather I stayed here with him."

"Would you do that?"

"Of course."

"All right, I'll be back shortly."

Susan dashed out the door and hurried to the parade ground where people were gathering. Libbie Custer was there with the other widows of her husband's unit. They already knew their men would not be returning, but they wanted to offer sympathy to the wives of Major Reno's men when they learned the fate of their husbands.

General Terry and Major Reno rode through the gate ahead of the wagons and the other mounted men. The crowd of women, children, and soldiers pressed close, searching for that one face dear to them.

There were happy tears for some, and as some women learned they were widows, there were tears of grief.

When Susan realized Thann was not riding with Terry and Reno, she searched for him among the wounded.

As the last wagon pulled inside and the gates were being shut, Susan was shocked to see Quiet Thunder riding beside a wagon, and Night Star and Gentle Fawn riding in the seat beside a soldier. She had no idea why they would be traveling with the Seventh Cavalry, but their faces were a welcome sight.

The Indians spotted Susan as she pushed through the crowd. Quiet Thunder was on the ground helping the women off the seat just as Susan reached them. While Quiet Thunder was lifting his mother down, Susan embraced Night Star and asked why they had come to the fort with the Seventh.

Before Night Star could answer, General Terry and Major Reno appeared, their faces grim.

Night Star kept an arm around Susan as they walked to her quarters. Amy Cowen hugged Susan and wept with her, then excused herself after being introduced to Susan's friends.

Quiet Thunder and Gentle Fawn held the papooses so that

Night Star could sit beside Susan and hold her hand. The Lord's peace and comfort was in Susan's heart, though she was shaken when she knew for sure that Thann was dead. While she vented her grief, Night Star spoke soft words of love and comfort.

Quiet Thunder told her how he and Thann had met amid the smoke of battle, and that it was Crazy Horse who shot Thann. He wept as he told her that his blood brother had died in his arms and that he had given him an honorable burial.

Quiet Thunder handed their little son to Night Star, then reached into the buckskin pouch at his waist and produced a silver medallion that matched the one he wore around his neck.

"John Stranger gave this to Thann the day he became a Christian, Susan," Quiet Thunder said. "I found it in his pocket. I know he would want you to have it."

Susan closed her fingers around the silver disk and pressed it to her breast. Tears spilled down her cheeks as she drew a shuddering breath and said, "Thank You, Lord Jesus, for John Stranger. Thank You that You sent him into Thann's life to lead him to Yourself. And thank You for the peace I have, knowing my beloved husband is there in heaven with You."

A baby's cry came from the back of the quarters, and Susan stood up. "Excuse me. It's time all of you met my son."

The Indian babies had been quiet through it all and were still behaving themselves when Susan came into the room, carrying her three-month-old baby.

"The only baby in this room whose name we all know is Blue Sky," Susan said with a smile. Then she sat down and turned to the handsome Oglala warrior. "Quiet Thunder," she began, "I want to thank you for being such a wonderful friend to Thann. Your blood-brother relationship was an important part of his life. When it came time to name our little son, he spoke of his love for you and asked if I would mind if we named our son after you."

A grin started to spread across Quiet Thunder's face.

"As far back as the Tyler family history can be traced, all the males have had a first name that started with *Th.*"

Quiet Thunder nodded.

Susan held her son for all to see. "I want you to meet Thunder Tyler!"

Quiet Thunder reached for his little namesake and hugged him close.

"Susan," Night Star said, "in one special way, Thann will live on right here on earth."

"How is that?"

Night Star's eyes misted. "When our little son was born, I wanted him to have a part of Quiet Thunder's name. Quiet Thunder wanted him to have part of his blood brother's name." She lifted the baby up and said, "Susan, meet Tyler Thunder!"

EPILOGUE

———◆———

In the weeks following the Little Bighorn battle, fresh troops were sent into the Black Hills area under the command of General Nelson A. Miles. The Sioux moved about, making themselves difficult to locate. In January 1877, Miles found the Oglala camp on the Tongue River when the snow was a foot deep. Red Cloud was not with them; Crazy Horse was in charge.

Miles attacked the camp, and the Oglalas were defeated. The survivors, including Crazy Horse, were scattered on the frozen plains without food and proper clothing.

Several months later, Crazy Horse and his people surrendered to General George Crook at a reservation in Nebraska. But Crazy Horse found that he could not endure reservation life. On September 5, 1877, he tried to escape and was killed by a soldier's bayonet.

On December 4, 1890, Indian policemen went on the Dakota reservation to arrest Chief Sitting Bull for embracing the dangerous Ghost Dance cult. His people tried to prevent his arrest. In the struggle the chief was shot dead.

For the rest of his life, Chief Red Cloud remained a forceful critic of white man's broken promises. He was so outspoken that the government agents in charge of the Oglalas attempted to depose him as chief of his people in 1881. The Oglalas would not stand for it, and he remained their chief until he died in 1909 on the Pine Ridge Reservation in South Dakota. He left behind these words:

> The white men made us many promises. More than I can remember. They never kept but one. They promised to take our land, and they took it.

OTHER COMPELLING STORIES BY
AL LACY

Books in the Battles of Destiny series:

☛ *A Promise Unbroken*

Two couples battle jealousy and racial hatred amidst a war that would cripple America. From a prosperous Virginia plantation to a grim jail cell outside Lynchburg, follow the dramatic story of a love that could not be destroyed.

☛ *A Heart Divided*

Ryan McGraw—leader of the Confederate Sharpshooters—is nursed back to health by beautiful army nurse Dixie Quade. Their romance would survive the perils of war, but can it withstand the reappearance of a past love?

☛ *Beloved Enemy*

Young Jenny Jordan covers for her father's Confederate spy missions. But as she grows closer to Union soldier Buck Brownell, Jenny finds herself torn between devotion to the South and her feelings for the man she is forbidden to love.

☛ *Shadowed Memories*

Critically wounded on the field of battle and haunted by amnesia, one man struggles to regain his strength and the memories that have slipped away from him.

☛ *Joy from Ashes*

Major Layne Dalton made it through the horrors of the battle of Fredericksburg, but can he rise above his hatred toward the Heglund brothers who brutalized his wife and killed his unborn son?

☛ *Season of Valor*

Captain Shane Donovan was heroic in battle. Can he summon the courage to face the dark tragedy unfolding back home in Maine?

Books in the Journeys of the Stranger series:

☞ *Legacy*

Can John Stranger bring Clay Austin back to the right side of the law...and restore the code of honor shared by the woman he loves?

☞ *Silent Abduction*

The mysterious man in black fights to defend a small town targeted by cattle rustlers and to rescue a young woman and child held captive by a local Indian tribe.

☞ *Blizzard*

When three murderers slated for hanging escape from the Colorado Territorial Prison, young U.S. Marshal Ridge Holloway and the mysterious John Stranger join together to track down the infamous convicts.

☞ *Tears of the Sun*

When John Stranger arrives in Apache Junction, Arizona, he finds himself caught up in a bitter war between sworn enemies: the Tonto Apaches and the Arizona Zunis.

☞ *Circle of Fire*

John Stranger must clear his name of the crimes committed by another mysterious—and murderous—"stranger" who has adopted his identity.

Books in the Angel of Mercy series:

☞ *A Promise for Breanna*

The man who broke Breanna's heart is back. But this time, he's after her life.

☞ *Faithful Heart*

Breanna and her sister Dottie find themselves in a desperate struggle to save a man they love, but can no longer trust.

☞ *Captive Set Free*

No one leaves Morgan's labor camp alive. Not even Breanna Baylor.

☞ *A Dream Fulfilled*

A tender story about one woman's healing from heartbreak and the fulfillment of her dreams.

Available at your local Christian bookstore